ALAN MARSHALL'S BATTLERS

ALAN MARSHALL'S BATTLERS

compiled by
GWEN HARDISTY

HYLAND HOUSE MELBOURNE

First published in 1983 by
Hyland House Publishing Pty Limited
23 Bray Street
South Yarra
Melbourne
Victoria 3141

National Library of Australia
cataloguing-in-publication data:

Marshall, Alan, 1902– .
  Alan Marshall's Battlers.

  ISBN 0 908090 58 7.

  I. Hardisty, Gwen. II. Title. III. Title:
  Battlers.

A828'.308

Jacket design by Jack Larkin
Typeset by ProComp Productions Pty Ltd, Adelaide
Printed by Globe Press, Brunswick

CONTENTS

KISSES A QUID A PIECE

'A QUID to anyone who can kiss this girl on the lips,' he yells from a platform in front of his tent. 'Come on lads, don't be frightened. She won't eat you.'

The girl looked tough.

'It's worth a quid to kiss you, sister,' some cove yelled from the back of the crowd.

'I only pay half price to rat-bags, brother. Ten bob to you,' she calls out.

I needed a quid. It looked easy to me. So I goes up to the platform. The cove welcomes me by beltin' a drum and yellin', 'Here's a contest. Here's a go.'

I had to get up on the boards. The girl looks sour at me. I'd been on the road for six weeks and had a seven day's growth.

'I can take it,' she says to the dame selling tickets.

'And I can dish it out,' I says to her.

'Don't hurt yourself,' she says.

After a stretch of sales talk we goes inside and the crowd fills the tent. I hadn't had a square meal for two days and was feelin' a bit weak on it.

I took off me coat and tightened me belt. Then the bloke gives another spout of talk and the girl comes at me dressed in bathing togs.

I sparred round a bit not knowing how to grab her. Then she dives at me and puts four grips on me at once. I didn't know whether I was comin' or goin'. I went over her shoulder somehow and landed flat on me back, behind her. She whips round but I wasn't gettin' up again till I got me wind.

I was fed up. I wished I hadn't come in. The crowd barracked me. I was crook on them. We got goin' again and I mixed it. I didn't like squeezin' her too hard. She was sorta soft. Then she put the Indian death-lock on me. She wasn't so soft. I forgot I was there to kiss her. I was fightin' to get away from her. I broke it and she got the splits on me. Hell! I was bein' busted.

'I give in,' I yells out and I taps the ground.

The crowd laughs. The boss says, 'You're there to kiss her, laddie. She's not after falls.'

I tries to drag myself to the door. She lets up and I stagger to me feet. She jumps at me then and throws me three times in four seconds. I was seein' things. I made a pass at her and she short-arm-jolted me. I couldn't find the door. She got me into an aeroplane spin and I thought I was in heaven, what with floatin' around. Then I hit the ground.

When I got up, north was east to me. I got mixed up in some arms and kissed a hairy mouth. It was the boss. He spun me round and I was tied up with her again.

I was smotherin', somehow. I bit into flesh and the girl jumps up holding her rump and swearing.

'You're here to kiss her mouth, laddie,' the boss says.

But I was all for the road again. I leaps for the door. She grabs me from behind and I feel the belt of me pants go. I grabs me pants and she gets me in a wrist lock. I had to let go me pants. I could hear bones crackin'.

I got goin'. I gave her all I had. But I didn't have enough. I wasn't fightin' for a kiss. I was fightin' for me life.

Me pants fell round me knees. She threw me over her head and me pants caught her round the neck. She fell wallop. I couldn't pull me pants up. They was caught under her chin. I struggled free. I jerked up me pants, grabbed me coat and just beat her to the door.

Did I keep going! Hell!

A quid a kiss! I'd earn it easier on a dairy farm.

RISING CHAMPION

THE pieman's hands were thrust deep in his pocket. His shoulders were hunched. He backed closer to the glowing door of his little oven.

Steam rising from the boiler gave back the glow of Neon lights. It wafted upwards into the frosty air like the red breath of a furnace.

The pony's harness jingled as he tossed his nosebag.

'Whoa, there,' said the pieman.

'What d'ya think of him now?' he asked.

He stamped his feet.

The man leaning against the cart did not take his eyes from the paper he was reading.

'I haven't finished it yet. He seems to be able to fight.'

He went on reading.

The pieman turned and looked at him. 'Seems to be,' he repeated scornfully. 'I tell you, Bob, he's a marvel. I'm not sayin' it because he's my own son. I'd say it no matter who he was.'

'Who'll have a pie?' he called out. He went on: 'I was there last night myself. He fights like I used to. Clip! Clip! an' the bloke's head flies back. Tap! Tap! an' the bloke's gasping.'

'Thirty pounds!' exclaimed the man. 'A good stake. There'll be some booze flying round tonight.'

'Not on your life, there won't,' said the pieman. 'Charlie's no boozer.

His companion looked at him with a slight smile.

'He's not like his old man, then,' he interrupted.

The pieman grunted. 'Well, no, Bob, he's not. I've trained him different.'

He rubbed his thick fingers slowly across his face as if recording the scars, the callouses, the broken nose, the thick ears that characterised it.

'Do you remember when you cracked that flash chap on the back of the head with a lump of lead-filled hose and got a hundred and ten pounds off him?' asked the man. 'In the Gardens, do you remember?'

The pieman laughed. He bent forward with mirth.

'A hundred and ten quid. An' I thought I'd be lucky if I got ten bob.' He suddenly grew serious. 'But I nearly did him in, Bob. The Jacks watched me for weeks.'

'The chap hasn't lived that could knock a cove out like you, Bill.'

'It's a fact, Bob.'

'I never ever hit a man twice,' he said.

'There was no need,' said the man.

'No,' said the pieman.

'But I've brought up Charlie different. I says to him, "Look, Charlie, look at me." I says, "if I'd saved my money, I wouldn't be selling pies today," I says. He's a great lad, Bob. He's a boxer, and he's going to be a champ. Money that's not honest is no good to him. I've trained him that way, see? Tonight he's coming into town to shove that thirty quid in the savings bank . . . What's for you, son?'

'A sav,' said the newsboy.

The pieman split a hot saveloy with a deft stroke of the knife. Steam rose from the pink meat. The newsboy drew a deep breath.

'Plenty of sauce,' said the boy.

'I say,' said the man, folding his paper. 'Isn't that your lad walking up the street.'

The pieman looked over his shoulder, the sauce bottle held aloft.

The pieman handed the boy his saveloy and roll, his eyes still searching the street.

'That's him,' he exclaimed, pleased. 'Look at his shoulders, Bob. Who's the cove he's with? It's not Dink Adams is it?' he asked anxiously. 'It is. That dirty crook Adams. We've worked together on jobs. Charlie doesn't know what sort of a chap he is, Bob.' Concern was in his face. 'He'd do him for his thirty quid before he knew what happened. Charlie's a boxer. He doesn't understand coves like that. He doesn't mix with crooks. I've trained him different.'

'They're going into the gardens,' said the man.

'Blow me, if they ain't,' exclaimed the pieman. 'I'll have to get Charlie out of this, Bob. Here, watch me cart.'

He pulled off his white apron.

'I'll give you half an hour,' said the man.

'I'll be back,' said the pieman.

He crossed the road at a half run.

At the entrance to the Gardens he paused, undecided. There was no one in sight. He set off down the darkest pathway. At the end he turned and retraced his steps slowly. He peered among the bushes with keen eyes.

A figure stepped out into the light.

'Charlie,' breathed the pieman.

'Why, Dad! What are you doing here? Look, I got a tenner off a mug I met in the street. He's lying there in the bushes.'

With a happy chuckle he waved a bundle of notes in front of the pieman's face.

'I cracked him with your old timer.'

He handed the pieman a length of leaded hose.

'I got it from your room. You take it home. I'll bank forty pounds tonight, Dad. Oh, boy!'

The pieman expelled a long breath.

'How many times did you have to hit him, Charlie?'

'Only once, Dad.'

The pieman placed his hand on his shoulder.

'Good lad,' he said.

THE NOBLE ART

His eight hundred pound car stood at the back of the tent. With a leather bag suspended from his neck he waited near the main entrance for the cue to appear on the platform. His boxing troupe was already there. There were six of them. There was a bearded wrestler. There was a negro. There was a Greek. The other three were Australian boxers discarded by the cities.

The high platform stood in front of the tent. Spread before it a country show crowd listened to the spruiker.

'Hurry. Hurry. Hurry,' he yelled through a megaphone.

The negro beat a drum. The Greek rang a bell. The others shouted an accompaniment. They flexed their muscles, drew deep breaths, thumped their chests.

The spruiker raised a hand. The bell and the drum snapped into silence.

'Is Sanders in the audience? Is the fighting farmer from Panabi here yet?'

He was there. He moved towards the platform. The crowd made way. They encouraged him with words. They called: 'Good on ya, Tom.' They gave advice: 'Go at him from the bell.' They were excited. They all knew him.

'Here he is,' bawled the spruiker. 'Here is your local champion . . . The fighting farmer from Panabi.' He broke into a savage, rhythmic chant accompanied by the wild boom and clang of drum and bell. 'The fighting farmer . . . the fighting farmer . . . the fighting farmer . . .'

It was time for the boss to appear. He had spent an hour

explaining to the local champion all that was required of him in exchange for the fiver he was to receive for taking part in this 'Fifty Pound Challenge'.

'Mix it for four rounds. You go down twice in the fifth, remember. In the sixth bring your left to his jaw and he'll go out to it. I'll be standing beside you on the platform when we are arguing. I'll give you all the answers under my breath. Cut up rough. We want to stir 'em up.'

The spruiker was trying to do this outside. 'Here's your local lad, Tom Sanders, who is to meet the heavyweight champion of Western Australia, Spike Peters, in a ten-round challenge for fifty quid.'

The boss appeared at the tent's entrance. The spruiker became a herald proclaiming the coming of a new Christ. 'Here comes Jack Stevens . . . Here comes Jack Stevens . . .' The negro joined him: The Greek—boom, boom, boom. 'Here comes Jack Stevens.' The bearded wrestler writhed in imaginary death-locks. 'Here comes Jack Stevens . . . *Jack Stevens* . . . STEVENS . . .'

The boss mounted the platform. He stood beside Tom Sanders. 'Now you know what you are taking on, lad.' He included the crowd by looking their way as he talked. 'Spike Peters is tough, and I might as well tell you, he's out to put you to sleep in the second round.'

'I'm not frightened of him.'

'Good on ya, Tom,' from a woman below them.

'I'll show him,' cried Tom uncertainly. He shook his fist in a show of truculence.

'Don't be so cocky,' warned the boss. 'He might show you something before you're finished.' He beckoned his man. 'Come up here, Spike.' The drum throbbed: The bell clanged.

Spike came forward. He had cauliflower ears. His face was misshapen. Spike was paid four pounds a week. He took part in six or seven fights between each pay. He was skilful. The ringcraft from years of experience was his. But Spike could take it. He had to take it. The local must always win. So Spike left openings in his guard and prayed that the deciding blow was according to his plea before each contest. 'When you throw it, see it's got no weight behind it.'

Jack Stevens, with a cupped hand to the side of his mouth, was stirring the crowd with announcements of merciless intention. He hinted at a grudge. Now 'a final settlement of differences.' But his voice was almost apologetic when he announced: 'Owing to the expense of staging this contest, admission will be three shillings.'

The opening of the tent doors was announced with a burst of sound. The crowd fought for admission . . . Three bob— Three bob—Three bob—to the tune of a hundred and fifty pound house. The big tent bulged with people. From his seat against a pole near the tent's centre, Spike watched them gloomily. They hadn't spent three bob for nothing. They wanted its equivalent in savagery. They wanted to see him staggering, dripping blood. They wanted to see him dazed, struggling to rise from the trampled ground. They wanted to see their farmer smash and pound him . . . And he had to see that they got what they wanted. He was paid four quid a week to take it, and take it again.

Jack Stevens strode over to him. He was the cold attendant of some huge machine whose parts were all that were present. At his gesture it would commence an inexorable movement that later would leave Spike prostrate on the ground.

Stevens raised a hand as he walked. It suggested a push. 'Back to the canvas, please. Stand back. Those in front, sit down. Back, please.'

He bent over Spike. His mouth was near Spike's ear. The words he spoke were commands and gave the lie to his solicitous hands which massaged and kneaded Spike's muscular arms and legs.

'Make it willing. Keep out of clinches. Hit low this round and I'll caution you. Let him belt you back into the crowd. Bump 'em. Get 'em excited. They'll hear 'em yellin' and we'll get more the next tent. Take one halfway through the sixth and see that it looks the goods.'

He took a watch from his pocket and stepped to the centre of the cleared space within the crowd. 'You all know Tom Sanders, your local champion. Give him a clap, boys. Put your hands together for the local lad.'

He hurried to the tent flap and held it open so that the applause could be heard outside. It was a signal for further beating of the drum. The bell clanged furiously. 'We're off. We're off,' yelled the spruiker.

Stevens returned to the tent centre. 'Shake hands,' he cried, his eyes on his watch.

Spike sprang from his seat. Tom met him halfway. Their gloves met in a perfunctory gesture of friendliness. They turned and strode apart, turned again and whipped into the conventional crouch.

'Time,' cried Stevens. He, too, crouched, following their movements with his bright, bird-of-prey eyes.

Spike was gliding after the wary, retreating Sanders. Sanders paused. Spike leapt in and drove short, rapid blows to his body. Sanders grunted then attacked furiously. Spike covered, waiting for the other to expend himself. He was in no hurry. But Tom's blows were hurting. Tom was trying to hurt him. Spike stepped back then slid in and mixed it savagely. Here's a taste of what I *could* do. He hammered Tom round the ring. Tom took a straight left on the jaw and went down. One-two-three. Stevens signalled the passing of each second with a conductor-like wave of the hand.

Tom got to his feet. He was nervous, uncertain. They moved, light-footed, round each other. Spike's eyes were hard. Spike had the bitterness.

'Hop into it. Fight, you big stiff.'

Spike suddenly drove Tom back among those who yelled. Umph. Umph. Smack.

'Look out!'

'Jesus!'

Tom snorted red breath.

'Break, blast you! Break!'

Stevens gave a frantic look at his watch. Ten seconds to go. 'Time,' he yelled.

Spike walked back to his corner. Stevens followed him with a towel across his shoulder. He massaged Spike's arms and snarled into his ear: 'Ease up, blast you! Take some from him.'

So Spike began to take it. He was paid four quid a week to take it.

Tom thrived on success. The crowd yelled their pleasure. Tom thought he was Joe Louis. He put all he had into his punches.

In the sixth round Spike gave him the opening. I'll move back with it, thought Spike. But Tom was too quick. A horse couldn't kick as hard as Tom hit Spike.

When Spike came round a quarter of an hour afterwards the tent was empty. He looked round then rested his head in his cupped hands.

Outside the spruiker was shouting, 'Can the bearded wrestler put the Indian death-lock on your local champion?'

Jack Stevens came in carrying a glass of water. Spike drained it. Stevens had a satisfied smile upon his face. He bent and patted Spike's shoulder. It was easy for him to bend to pat Spike's shoulder because the bag of money pulled his head down.

'An extra quid in your envelope this week,' said Stevens. 'An extra quid for you, boy.'

'SIX SAUSAGES IS NOTHING'

THE man set a match to the wood. The flames licked the blackened billies he had filled in the creek. He unrolled a newspaper parcel and revealed, lying on a damp, inner covering, a flaccid coil of sausages.

The two little girls were unrolling the tent. From within its folds they had taken blankets, woollen gowns and jumpers over which they argued, rejecting this and claiming that in anticipation of the cold night they had been told to expect.

At the sound of the rustling paper they ceased their bargaining and ran over to the fire.

Joan was short and fat. She ran with long, slow strides, landing heavily on her heel at the conclusion of the forward thrust of each leg. Winona clutched three parrot feathers in her hand. She was 'saving feathers'.

'There should be fifteen, uncle. Is there?'

The man handled the sausages experimentally. He gazed at them with interest as if they were rare and unusual objects. He pressed them with a fork, wondering at the toughness of the skin.

'They look as if they had just died,' commented Winona, peering over her uncle's shoulder.

'There'll be five each,' announced Joan triumphantly, after a swift calculation.

'Good Heavens!' exclaimed the man, astounded at the figure. He looked at Joan reflectively. 'I suppose she could,' he murmured to himself.

He held them up in a long plaited string and proceeded

to count them. 'Fifteen! By Jove, you're right!' he said.

'Five each,' exclaimed Joan, rubbing her hands.

'And a bottle of sauce,' said Winona.

'I doubt whether I could eat five,' said the man thoughtfully. 'Not if we are going to eat anything else.'

'Then I can have six,' said Joan, delighted.

'Steady,' said the man.

'Six sausages is nothing,' said Joan.

'We won't eat bread with them,' said Winona. 'We're not home now.'

'Anyway, there's no bread,' said Joan.

'Pity your mother made a mistake about that service car,' said the man. 'It doesn't pass here till midnight. I was lucky to be able to buy these sausages and the bottle of sauce.'

'Will the man leave our tucker box by the side of the road?' asked Winona.

'Yes. Under that big tree,' said the man. 'We will get it in the morning.'

He raked an open space among the coals and pushed a cast-iron griller into the glow.

The sausages sizzled as they were placed on the hot metal. Meat slowly swelled and burst from the end of one of them.

'Look at that, now,' said Joan.

'They never do that at home,' said Winona.

The man poked at the sausage. The round lump of meat became detached and fell into the fire.

'A little one for somebody,' complained Joan. 'It's lost half its meat.'

Fat spluttered from the sausages. They began to shrink.

'They're getting smaller and smaller,' said Joan anxiously.

'How do you know when they are done?' muttered the man.

He prodded a sausage with a fork. It slipped into the receptacle at the foot of the griller, now filled with boiling fat. There was a splutter. The man yelled and thrust his finger into his mouth. A dislodged sausage fell into the fire.

'Did you burn yourself, uncle?' asked Winona.

'A sausage short for someone,' commented Joan.

The man withdrew his finger and shook his hand in the air.

'Are you swearing, uncle?' asked Joan.

'No,' said the man. He examined his finger.

'The sausages are getting smaller and smaller,' warned Joan.

'Cripes!' said the man.

He began a hurried attack on the sausages, spearing them with a fork and flicking them on to three enamel plates resting beside the fire.

'There goes another one,' said Joan. The sausages hissed on the coals.

'Grab it quick,' cried Winona.

'Five for me and four for you, now,' said Joan resignedly. The sausage became engulfed in ashes.

'Eat them while they are hot,' ordered the man. He continued retrieving sausages from the griller. The plates were hidden by clusters of them.

'Oo!' exclaimed Joan. 'Look at them. I've never ever had enough sausages before in my life. And as much sauce as we like, too.'

They smothered their laden plates with the thick, red liquid and began eating.

'Gee!' exclaimed Joan ecstatically. 'We haven't got to eat bread or anything. Just sausages.'

At 2 a.m. the man rose from a bed he had made at the foot of a sapling and walked over to the fire. He replenished it with logs and crouched close to the flames. He drew his dressing gown tighter around him and looked over his shoulder as if the cold were a tangible thing attacking him from the rear.

He suddenly turned his glance on to the little white tent erected between two trees and sat motionless, listening. He rose and, walking over to the tent, drew back the flap. He fumbled for matches and lit the hurricane lamp suspended from the ridge pole.

'What is the matter, Winona?' he asked. Winona was sitting up amid her blankets, crying. 'Is the ground hard?'

'I'm sick,' she sobbed.

'Sick!' exclaimed the man in dismay.

Joan had raised herself on to an elbow. She was wearing

a red jumper that had been made for an adult. Her hands were lost in its sleeves.

'She's got a pain in her stomach,' she explained, 'and my stomach feels funny, too.'

'Cripes,' said the man. He sat down on a log pulled into the tent for a seat.

The two children looked at him, confident that he would take direct and effective action. Winona had stopped crying.

'How do you mean, sick?' asked the man looking at Winona. He was sparring for time.

'I feel full,' she said.

'Full,' exclaimed the man. 'Well, what's wrong with that?'

'But I feel sick full.'

'I feel as if I'd like to be sick,' Joan joined in.

'Like to be!' exclaimed the man.

'Want to be, then,' explained Joan.

'That's nearly as bad,' said the man.

'Is it?' said Joan, a little weakly.

'Have you got pains?' asked the man.

'Oh, yes!' they both explained, glad to be on common ground.

'I think you had both better go outside the tent and put a finger down your throat.'

'Will that make you better?' asked Joan eagerly.

'Yes.'

'I will, then.'

'I'll wait till you do,' said Winona.

Joan rose from among the blankets. After some trouble her hand emerged from the long, red sleeve and grasped the top of her pyjama trousers. She walked out into the light of the camp fire.

She came back very quickly.

'Feel any better now?' asked the man.

'I feel worse,' she said. 'I had a hard job to keep from being properly sick.'

'What!' exclaimed the man.

'If I hadn't pulled my finger out I'd have been sicker'n I am.'

She crawled back beneath the blankets.

'I knew it would make you worse,' said Winona. 'I did it once and it was awful.'

The man's eyes suddenly became fixed and introspective.

'What is the matter, uncle?' asked Winona.

'Gosh! I believe it's coming on me.'

A gurgle of laughter came from the two girls. They suddenly felt much better. They watched their uncle with pleasurable concern.

'How do you feel now?' asked Winona.

'Like nothing on earth,' said the man.

'You only had four sausages,' said Joan.

'And a third of a bottle of sauce,' said Winona.

The man jumped to his feet and rushed outside.

The sun had just risen when they finished washing in the creek.

'We won't eat much this morning,' said the man, drying his face. 'We will go up and collect our tucker box and then we will come back and boil three eggs.'

'Mother said she would put the eggs on top,' said Joan.

'Good,' said the man.

With their faces glowing from the sting of cold water they walked slowly up the track to the main highway.

Beneath an old gum by the side of the road rested a narrow, wooden box.

'Hooray!' called the man.

The girls ran forward, anxious to open it. Joan unfastened a catch and lifted the hinged lid. A letter lay on top of the contents, pinned to a large formless parcel.

'A letter from Mum,' cried Winona. 'Read it, uncle.'

He read it aloud.

'Dear Uncle, Joan and Winona —

I know what you three love best in the world — sausages. I'm enclosing three pounds. Have a good time, all of you. — Mother.'

THE NIGHT WE HAD VISITORS

IT WAS six o'clock. Our visitors were expected any minute. Joan, Winona and I stood in the dining-room looking at the table.

Their mother had excelled herself. The cutlery gleamed; the white cloth glowed with pride; the bowl of flowers in the centre was a masterpiece of artistic arrangement.

'This'll knock 'em,' I said, rubbing my hands.

'Knock who, uncle?' asked Joan.

I changed my chain of thought.

'Look, Joan,' I said. 'Your mother said you are to behave yourself tonight. No asking for two helpings of ginger pudding unless there's enough left over and the visitors have had a return. And don't forget to say the person's name when you are introduced. Smile and say: "How are you, Mr Woodhouse? How are you, Mrs Woodhouse? How are you, Miss Woodhouse?"'

'I don't very much want to know how any of them are,' said Joan.

'Even if you don't,' I said, 'that's what you say.'

'And,' said Winona, joining forces with me, 'you'll have to talk sense tonight. No talking about: "the cat was at the birds last night", or "how is the sick chook, grandfather?"'

'Fancy you talking,' said Joan. 'You're always talking about that sissy, Minnie Birtles . . .'

Their mother interrupted.

'Remember, all of you, this is a clean cloth. If you spill any soup tonight, Joan, I'll put paper in front of you tomorrow.'

'Soup! Hurray!' cried Winona.

'Don't you go talking like that when the visitors come,' I said. 'They will think we never have soup.'

'Neither we do,' said Joan. 'Well, not very often.'

'Well, you've got to act as if we do,' I said.

'Grandfather is sure to say something,' said Joan.

'You watch yourself,' I said. 'Grandfather is all right.'

There was a ring at the door. We all sprang into action. Joan and Winona fled. Their mother snatched off her apron. I went to the door.

Miss Woodhouse was a very pretty girl. She had fluffy hair and she said 'delicious' and 'scrumptious' and 'gorgeous'. Mr Woodhouse was a businessman with more money than the king. Mrs Woodhouse was just Mrs Woodhouse.

It was very important that I make an impression on Miss Woodhouse. That is if I wanted to get on in the world.

Joan and Winona were introduced. Joan, remembering my instructions, kept a fixed smile on her face. After repeating, 'How are you?' three times with parrot-like precision, she looked at me for approval. I gave it with a weak smile. Miss Woodhouse was watching me.

Grandfather had difficulty in 'catching' the name.

'Woodhouse,' I said slowly and distinctly.

'What sort of house?' queried grandfather with his ear cupped in his hand.

Joan regarded it as her special privilege to enlighten grandfather on all matters in which his hearing was a handicap.

'Wood,' she yelled at him. 'W-double O-D. Like what you chop.'

Mr Woodhouse laughed without enthusiasm.

'Yes—ah—that is, yes,' he said.

Grandfather shook hands with him. He shook hands with them all. He then became conversational as befitted a receiver of guests.

'I see in Americy weatherboard houses are coming back into favour,' he said.

Dinner was announced.

Grandfather and I stood behind our chairs waiting for the guests to be seated.

'Sit down, uncle,' said Joan expansively. 'You're always first down other nights.'

I forced a laugh. 'These children,' I murmured.

We started the soup from an even break, Joan taking the lead after the fourth spoonful.

Grandfather raised his head and informed our visitors that he couldn't remember when he had tasted vegetable soup last.

Joan gave me a startled look as from one of two conspirators betrayed. She made a valiant effort to correct the impression created by grandfather's lapse.

'Why, we often have it, don't we, uncle?'

'Of course,' I replied with a fine indifference.

Joan frowned at grandfather as a warning against further indiscretions.

She finished her soup by pursuing the last drop round the plate with great industry. She welcomed the roast with almost audible sounds of appreciation and, glancing at my plate, commented:

'You haven't got the outside tonight, uncle.'

'Please take mine,' exclaimed Mr Woodhouse, holding his plate towards me. 'I have evidently been served with your portion.'

'Not at all,' I protested. 'Joan is having one of her little jokes.' I dismissed it airily. 'Don't take any notice of her, Mr Woodhouse.'

'You are such a happy family,' said Mrs Woodhouse benignly.

'We weren't so happy this morning when Joan broke the O off uncle's typewriter,' said Winona.

'It hasn't hurt it,' defended Joan. 'Uncle uses the Q and rubs out the tail.'

'Can you type?' Miss Woodhouse asked me.

'I get on quite well, Miss Woodhouse,' I answered. 'I do all my own typing.'

'It must make your finger tired, uncle,' said Joan.

'He uses two,' Winona came to my aid.

Miss Woodhouse quickly changed the conversation.

'Has anyone seen Deanna Durbin in *Three Smart Girls*

Grow Up?' she asked. 'I was simply transported last night.'

'Transported,' echoed Joan. 'That's what one of our relations was.'

'Would you like another helping, Mr Woodhouse?' I rushed in to ask.

The pudding came at last—the ginger pudding. Joan and Winona sat stiffly erect while it was being served. With great restraint they waited till the guests had begun eating, then rushed in to make up for lost time.

They finished first and sat before their empty plates watching the progress of the Woodhouse family.

Grandfather, after laying down his empty spoon, looked at Joan and asked: 'Are you going to have some more pudding, Joan?' It was a request for a partner.

'I don't know yet, grandfather,' yelled Joan. 'I'll tell you in a minute.'

This statement effectively ruled out the Woodhouse family for a second lap.

Joan, grandfather and Winona finished the pudding.

Joan ended the meal with a slice of bread and butter.

'Do you like bread and butter, Joan?' asked the astounded Mrs Woodhouse.

'I always like to finish up with something that doesn't make my mouth water for more,' explained Joan.

I rose and conducted our guests into the living-room, leaving the two girls sitting meditatively before the stricken table.

I returned for cigarettes.

'How'd I do, uncle?' whispered Joan eagerly.

'WHAT'S THE TIME?'

I WAS in the bathroom shaving. Joan burst in. She was in pyjamas.

'What's the time, uncle?'

I looked at my wrist watch.

'Eight o'clock,' I said.

'Oo!' said Joan. She bolted, calling from the hall, 'Mum, what'll I wear today?'

'Put on the dress you wore yesterday,' came a voice from the kitchen.

'It's got ink on it,' yelled Joan.

'Be quiet,' said Winona from the bedroom. 'You'll wake grandfather.'

'Grandfather can't hear anything,' said Joan.

'Hurry, Joan,' called her mother. It's a quarter-past eight.'

'A quarter-past eight!' exclaimed Joan in consternation. 'Uncle says it's eight,' she cried.

I stopped shaving and opened the bathroom door. 'My watch is right,' I said firmly.

Joan ran into grandfather's bedroom.

'What's the time by your watch, grandfather?' she yelled.

There was an interval in which grandfather struggled from the depths.

'Eh!' he said.

'What's the time by your watch, grandfather?' Deafness was no proof against Joan's voice.

'My glasses . . .' began grandfather.

Joan charged from the room crying. 'Where's grandfather's glasses?'

I again opened the bathroom door.

'Don't you wake grandfather, Joan.'

'He's awake,' she said. 'I just asked him the time.'

'My watch is on the table,' said grandfather to himself, but Joan heard him. She darted back.

'I'll look for your glasses tonight, grandfather.' She seized his watch. 'Ten past eight,' she cried unbelievingly. 'Your watch is mad, grandfather,' she cried.

'Eh!' quavered grandfather; but Joan was already in her bedroom struggling with the inky dress.

'Who's going to feed the canaries?' asked Winona.

'I've no time,' said Joan. 'There's plenty of seed on the floor of their cage. Canaries haven't got very big stomachs.'

'Joan and Winona, hurry up,' came from the kitchen. 'Your porridge is getting cold.'

'It's my turn to have the milk off the top of the bottle,' said Winona.

'Where's my other shoe?' cried Joan.

'I saw the pup chewing your shoe in the washhouse,' I informed her.

She disappeared in the direction of the washhouse in a hopping, one-sided run.

I washed my razor under the running tap, then looked sorrowfully in the mirror at the razor-sore skin on my throat.

Joan opened the door. 'What's the time, uncle?'

'Ten past eight.'

'The clock in the kitchen says twenty-five past eight,' complained Joan. 'I know I'll be late.'

'Get the right time from the wireless,' I suggested.

'Tell uncle his bacon is getting cold, and you children hurry up.' The voice from the kitchen was becoming more dictatorial.

'Your bacon is getting cold, uncle,' said Joan, wetting her hands under the running water and placing them against her face.

She dried herself vigorously as if she had just finished an extensive and thorough wash. She looked down at her shoe, her face twisted in distaste.

'My shoe is wet with pup spit,' she said.

'Yes,' I said abstractedly. 'Razor blades—razor blades—

one shilling—and a bottle of ink. I mustn't forget.'

'There's ink on my dress,' said Joan.

'Hurry up.' The person in the kitchen was certainly a dictator.

'What's the time, uncle?'

'A quarter-past eight.'

'History today,' complained Joan. 'I know when the Romans landed in Britain, but not much else.'

'When did they land,' I asked.

'Ten sixty-six.'

'Good,' I said.

Joan went out and in a minute the wireless blared forth a march that shook the house to its foundations. Every inside door opened with a jerk, while the projected heads cried with one voice:

'Turn off that wireless! You'll wake grandfather!'

The wireless flicked off as if murdered with an axe. Joan scurried into the hall as if pursued by enemies. She disappeared into grandfather's room.

'Grandfather,' she yelled. 'The wireless won't keep you awake, will it?'

'Eh!' grandfather said vaguely.

'You don't mind the wireless on, do you?' Joan shouted.

'No,' said grandfather.

Encouraged by this authority Joan informed the entire household in a shouted proclamation that: 'Grandfather says it is all right.'

She again turned on the wireless, but in a softer tone. She listened to the strains of music, then switched to another station. The house became filled with bursts of opera interspersed with the wail of crooners, weather forecasts and advertisements for breakfast foods.

'Housewives know . . . I love my sweetie . . . rain with cold winds . . . Pom, pom, pom-pom-pom . . .'

Joan gave up the search in disgust.

'You never know the time they give you the time,' she announced at the breakfast table, where Winona and I had divided the newspaper into two, her part containing Mickey Mouse and mine, Professor Nimbus.*

* A comic strip.

'What is the time now, uncle?'

'Half-past eight.'

'I'm going by you,' she said. 'The clock says a quarter-to-nine, but, mind you, uncle, I'm going by you.'

It was a heavy responsibility.

We discussed the scanty milk allowance, the scarcity of porridge, how much grandfather was likely to eat and the appetite of canaries.

'What's the time now, uncle?'

'A quarter-to-nine.'

It seemed satisfactory. Joan rose leisurely, read Mickey Mouse, assured her mother she had a hanky, had washed her face, polished her shoes, brushed her hair, cleaned her teeth, put the cockatoo out in the sun and fed the canaries, but was careful not to state the day each had occurred.

Winona switched on the wireless.

'Stand by for the nine o'clock time signal.'

There was a release of furious action and lamentation. Joan seemed to be in three places at once. She appeared, running strongly, at different parts of the house collecting books, bags, a hat, odd pencils, a ruler . . . while loading me with recrimination and reproach.

A chair fell over, the back door slammed, the dog barked, the pup yelped, the cockatoo announced in a senile croak, 'Uncle is mad.'

'Goodbye, Mum.'

Bang went the back gate.

Joan had left for school.

THOSE WHO WALK THIS STREET

THOSE who walk this street at night sometimes paused at the cafe door. The square of light that carpeted the footpath was a refuge from darkness, a resting place on journeys to homes hidden in narrow alleys or behind veranda fences smoothed by the folded arms and resting breasts of women.

The light was warm with the smell of hamburgers, of grilled steak and eggs, of buttered toast. It emphasised the unfriendliness of the divided darkness so that some of those who loitered, freed of uncertainty, stepped through the door and sat at the tables lining the wall.

The proprietress of the cafe was a Polish woman. She had broad hips and wore a short dress that gave her the appearance of a bell. She did not address her patrons as individuals, her remarks were to them all.

'Are you all served now? Who wants more toast?'

She sang to herself as she strode between the tables and sometimes executed a dancing movement when turning.

'La, la; la-la-la. Fried eggs for one.'

Her husband prepared the orders behind a low counter at the end of the room. He was a big man with the disturbed expression of one who wrestles with a problem. As each customer rose to go he called out, 'Goodbye dere', and smiled at them self-consciously.

The customers often called across the room to him and his wife.

'Has Sam been in tonight, Pete?'

'No. Not here tonight. Friday night maybe.'

'All I want's a cup of tea, Daise.'

'Goodo Rube.'

Ruby always sat at the table that faced the door, a cup of tea before her, her eyes half closed against the rising smoke of a cigarette. She was a stout middle-aged woman with a shapeless body and short fingered hands. Beneath one of the rayon stockings that clothed her legs could be seen the spiralling ridge of a bandage. She watched the men who entered, her regard expressing no anticipation. The baby resting on the shoulder of the blackfellow sitting with his back to Ruby at the next table, sucked its fist contentedly. One plump arm, deeply creased at wrist and elbow, hung down his back. Its deep set, brown eyes gazed at Ruby with a steady insistence.

When the little man with the black overcoat entered he turned from the pressure of Ruby's regard and sought a table where the sudden tumult of his thoughts could be met with reason. He moved a chair but quickly replaced it and walked over to the table where she sat, her face veiled behind a wavering film of smoke.

He seated himself before her, then leant across the table as if that which he was about to whisper was urgent, secret and necessary.

She did not welcome him. She watched him speculatively, sucking at her cigarette so that it no longer drooped but projected rigidly from her lips.

The chair upon which he sat pressed against the back of the one occupied by the blackfellow. The baby clutched its father's thick hair and raised itself higher on his shoulder. It reached towards the little man and beat its wet hand upon him. The man turned quickly and for a moment faced the baby who smiled at him and waited with suspended arm for some words of approval.

But the man's gaze was abstracted and he did not recognise the baby's desire to play. He turned away from it and continued his urgent questioning.

The baby grew pensive. It raised its hand to its open mouth but its sense of direction went astray and its fist came to rest against its cheek. It turned its head till its mouth found the hand. It sucked happily.

In a moment the man rose and left the cafe. Ruby remained at the table, but her expression had softened. She noticed the baby.

'Hullo dearie. Tch, tch, there's a dear. Tch, tch.' She waved as she spoke.

The baby did not withdraw its hand from its mouth but it slowly smiled at her.

The Polish woman, sweeping the smell of fried onions across the tables as she passed, struck a pose with a laden plate held aloft.

'Who ordered onions?'

'Right,' called a young man from a table near the door. He was a Greek and was dressed in khaki uniform. 'That's for me.'

The Polish woman placed it before him with a flourish.

'La, la; la-la-la. Two bob.'

She glanced through the doorway as she took the money, then called back over her shoulder.

'Your gentleman friend is at the door, Rube.'

Ruby rose and walked to the entrance. The little man with the black overcoat had returned. He spoke to her and they both moved into the cafe. He was holding a pound note in his hand.

'Have you got change of a quid, Daise?' Ruby asked.

The Polish woman was still standing beside the Greek. She called to her husband.

'Got change of a quid, Pete?'

The husband stepped from behind the counter and walked over to the group.

'I don't know,' he said, frowning as he opened the small chamois purse he had taken from his pocket.

'All silver it will be.'

'I can change it,' said the Greek rising from his chair. 'I got a ten bob note.'

He took the money from his pocket and counted out ten shillings in silver which he placed on a ten shilling note. He handed the money to the little man who gave the pound note in exchange.

A strange silence had entered the cafe. The clatter of knives and forks had ceased. The customers sat without moving watching the five people standing near the door.

'See you tomorrow, Daise,' said Ruby.

'Goodnight Rube,' said the Polish woman.

'Goodbye dere,' said her husband.

The man in the black overcoat took Ruby by the arm and they walked out through the door into the darkness.

The three who were left standing watched them go. Upon the face of the Polish woman, upon the face of her husband, and upon the face of the Greek there was a smile like that which sometimes rests on those who watch little children at play.

The Polish woman turned and faced the silence behind her as if in all those watching faces there was a question.

'It is her first break for a long time,' she said.

THE OLD WOMAN AND THE DOGS

THEY did not know she was mad. When she looked at them her eyes lost that wild, unfettered gleam, and became calm and gentle.

There were seven of them. They had no names. She called them all 'Deary'. They were of no particular breed. Their origin was a mystery. They had passed her gate in their wanderings. They had been hungry, and she had fed them. They had been tired, and she had given them beds of bags to lie upon.

She had stroked their heads with thin, old fingers, and talked softly to them. So they lived with her.

Sometimes her voice became loud and excited. She waved her arms. She stood upright with wisps of tired, grey hair athwart her forehead. She swayed upon her feet.

Then they leaped around her barking, thinking it was a game she played.

But when she sank to the floor in the dark corner, muttering and plucking at her face with frightened fingers, they gathered round her in silence.

The backyard was very small. They often became irritable one with the other, and sometimes they fought. She was possessed of amazing strength, and pulled them apart with loud cries.

Each morning she took them for a walk. The preparation was full of barkings, leapings and the patterings of excited feet on the kitchen floor.

Four she held on leash. Three ran free. Each dog had to take his turn on the lead.

They strained at the ropes, but the old woman held the ropes very tightly in her hand, and although the dogs arched their backs and held their heads low and slipped and scratched on the gravelly road, they only succeeded in quickening her stride, for she leant back using her weight to help stay them.

Thus her progress up the street was almost a triumphant one, heralded, as it was, by her loud cries and those of her subjects.

But sleepy-eyed housewives bending to pick up bottles of milk said to themselves, 'There goes the mad woman and her dogs. Poor thing.'

In a street of gum trees an Australian terrier stopped and watched their approach. His little heart beat fast. They barked so much. There were so many of them. He turned, and began running.

But three dogs overtook him with a rush, so that he propped desperately, and stopped crouched against the fence.

A big untidy dog, with erect tail wagging and pricked ears upon a stiff-necked, eager head, stepped forward and stood before him. He whined, and Bluey, feeling comforted, raised his head and their noses met.

The big dog barked. He sank on his chest to the pavement, his front legs flattened each side of him, his hind ones still unbent. He suddenly whirled in a circle and resumed his unnatural position. Bluey wanted to romp with him, but the old woman was near and the barking of the dogs she held roused in him a further panic. He fled. The three dogs followed.

He pressed close to the fence as he ran. The twigs and leaves of hedges projecting between pickets brushed his coat as he passed.

But the dogs crowded on him so that he stopped, and in a sudden abjectness of spirit he turned upon his back, his four feet held pathetically aloft as if to plead with them.

They stood before him desiring to be friendly, but the cries of the old woman recalled them, and they left him.

He got to his feet. The old woman stopped. Their eyes met. Under her strange, wide-eyed, comforting glance Bluey's trembling left him. He yearned towards her and the security she promised.

But she called her dogs again, and they continued their walk.

Bluey trotted penitently behind them unnoticed by the old woman. But at a corner she saw him. She stayed her dogs. Again they looked at each other.

''Ere, Deary,' she said.

At first he missed his bed of cushions and his regular meals. He became unkempt and often scratched himself. But he gained great courage and contentment.

He learned the rules which governed their works. He always returned to her feet when she called him, and, when tired, she sat resting on some convenient step, he lay his head on her ragged lap, regarding her reverently.

A man sauntered into that street of trees one day. He smoked a pipe, the bowl of which he held in his hand. He breathed the air of the morning with delight, and often stopped to gaze at cats that sunned themselves on gate posts or licked their glossy fur on narrow verandas.

There came a clamour and a shouting, a wild tumult. The cats fled with arched backs. Like Boadicea encharioted, the old woman and her tugging dogs surged over a rise. Quietness fled from beneath the trees.

The man took his pipe from his mouth and gazed unbelievingly at the approaching cavalcade.

Bluey, with three companions, ran free. They explored each drain with delighted tails. They cleared the road of cats, and announced the approach of their benefactress with a constant yapping.

The man gazed at Bluey with a comical expression of incredulity and excitement. 'Bluey!' he cried. 'Hey, Bluey! Here.'

Bluey leaped round at the sound. He barked, and ran joyfully towards him.

''Ere, Deary. 'Ere. Come 'ere,' called the old woman.

He stopped.

'Bluey,' cried the man.

Bluey looked from one to the other, quivering and whining with uncertainty.

''Ere, Deary.'

With sudden resolution he turned and trotted back to the old woman. He leaped to her hand, resting his little front legs against her torn skirt. She bent and patted him.

Bluey turned and trotted proudly in front of her. He led her past the man and his pipe. Like a dignitary upon which has been conferred the greatest of honours, he looked neither to the right nor the left in his passing. He was filled with a great pride.

I LOOK BACK

So THIS is the last issue of *The Guardian.* I'm sorry. It made its mistakes. It had its troubles. But it always came back fighting. It fought for truth and justice and a better life for all of us. It was a courageous paper.

I owe it a lot. I cut my writing teeth in the pages of *The Workers' Voice*, the name of *The Guardian* in the days when the wages of a girl starting in a boot factory was 12/6d a week.

Those were the days of the depression and I spent a lot of time wandering the streets. I was not politically conscious, and imagined in my innocence that articles describing the conditions under which people were forced to live would be welcomed by the daily press. I was mixing with hungry, despairing men and I wrote a series of reportage pieces in which I attempted to describe the tragedy of their existence.

I couldn't place them until someone mentioned *The Workers' Voice.* I tried this paper and thus began a relationship that gave me an opportunity to develop any writing ability I possessed, and to say what I wanted to say. The articles appeared under the heading of 'Proletarian Picture Book' and became a weekly feature.

They were exciting times. The battles fought by *The Workers' Voice* embraced all the aspects of the struggles then taking place. Those I remember most vividly, those in which *The Workers' Voice* played a leading role, were struggles in which I was involved and which represented signposts in my life.

In 1934, I was stirred into action by the Government's

treatment of Egon Erwin Kisch, a Czech writer, who was barred from landing in Australia where he was going to address a meeting against war and fascism. He had been a victim of Hitler's persecution in Germany where, even then, concentration camps were being set up.

Finally he jumped from his ship on to the pier at Port Melbourne and broke his leg. Kisch was a writer, and his arrest became the concern of all Australian writers who valued freedom.

He was released, and I heard him address a huge meeting at the West Melbourne Stadium, where I first learnt of nazi torture and the horror its victims were suffering.

Count Felix von Luckner's visit to Australia in 1938 started a series of demonstrations which culminated in mounted police charging crowds of demonstrators in Victoria Street. The police did not discriminate. Women were batoned as well as men, and there were a number of arrests.

Von Luckner, a nazi spy, featured in the press as a personality figure whose strength was such that he would tear telephone books in half, was a dyed-in-the-wool nazi who even then was preparing for the war that was soon to break out in Europe. Yet he was presented as a hero. It was *The Workers' Voice* which showed him up in his true colours.

General Motors about this time was preparing to introduce a speed-up system which would have turned workers into machines. I managed to obtain a book of instructions which was issued to foremen who were supposed to familiarise themselves with its contents.

It was an astounding book, which gave a minimum time for all movements necessary in the simplest tasks. While the right hand was screwing a nut, the left hand had to be engaged in an equally productive task. .05 of a second to extend the arm, .06 to do something else—everything was timed to a fraction of a second. The system, we were told, had the blessing of the Duke of Windsor.

I wrote three articles exposing this speed-up system. When *The Workers' Voice*, in which they were featured, appeared, hundreds of copies were sold outside the gates of General Motors. The system was not put into operation.

The visit of the Italian cruiser *Raimondo Montecuccoli* to Melbourne in 1938 was an occasion in which *The Workers' Voice* exposed the sinister activities of the fascists aboard. An Italian taxi driver who had gone aboard with hundreds of other visitors, was seized and held prisoner on the ship. The demonstrations that took place in protest against the seizure of this man were the largest Melbourne had seen to that time.

Thousands of people collected along the Port Melbourne waterfront. The pier where the Italian cruiser was berthed, was barred to visitors. The huge crowd paraded the waterfront shouting their anger across the water from where answering shouts could be heard.

'Taffy' Orlando, the taxi driver, had been bashed unconscious, and was in danger of being abducted to Italy. However, continued demonstrations succeeded in having him released. It was *The Workers' Voice* which kept the public supplied with the facts that would otherwise have been suppressed.

I wonder does anyone remember Dick Waitley? He fought in Spain with the International Brigade, and lectured on his experiences at the Writers' League, of which I was then president. He was a shrunken man, shy and awkward, and when speaking gave the impression of trying to efface himself. Yet on that night when he spoke at the Writers' League, he held us in silence by the force of his personality. We rose and gave him a standing ovation.

One of the best journalists *The Workers' Voice* ever had was Jim Crawford. He was a fine writer and an honest one. We interviewed the Red Dean together. Jim was so thorough he left me with nothing to say.

'What songs did your mother sing to you when you were a little boy?' I asked the Dean. I was searching for a new angle.

He leant back in his chair, smiled, and sang a little song about a mouse.

When we were leaving Jim said: 'I think that song revealed a lot. He is a great man.'

The trial of Frank Hardy at the end of the forties was given a complete cover in *The Guardian*, as it had by then become. With its help, the Frank Hardy Defence Committee was able to raise the necessary money to defend him. Hardy showed remarkable courage in this trial, the result of which is now history.

I have only mentioned a few of the outstanding events of the last thirty-three years, but this is evident: though *The Workers' Voice* was subject to the most unscrupulous and vicious attacks for the stand it took in each of these events, history has proved it was right.

In the light of this fact it is interesting to speculate what history will say of *The Guardian*'s fight against conscription, of its stand against the terrible war in Vietnam where a country is being decimated and a people destroyed in a courageous defence of their freedom.

As in the past, history will prove *The Guardian* to be right.

Farewell *The Guardian*. You retire undefeated.

AUSTRALIAN PICTURE-BOOK I

THEY call it 'Collingwood Coke'.

At five o'clock when the boot factories are silent, ragged children pull their billy carts up back alleys and streets to wait patiently at rear doors for its distribution. Waste pieces of leather from the cutting of soles is swept into bags and kept for them. Their meals are cooked over it, their thinly-clad bodies are warmed by it, the air above their homes is tainted by the smell of its burning.

From the backs of cattle fattened on the estates of rich Australian land-owners it passes on to agents and tanners, leaving with each some share of its wealth until the discarded and mutilated remains smoulder out warmth from the fire-places of the Collingwood poor.

His face was thin like a cry from a deep well.

He stood in the mouth of a large galvanised iron funnel and sprayed gold paint on to strips of wood that would some day form the frames of pictures. From the neck of the funnel came a deep roar like a train in the night. A fan concealed behind the cavity sucked the gold mist from around him so that sometimes one could see him quite clearly standing there.

The room in which he worked was at the far end of the Brunswick mill so that the heavy, sickly smell of his paint could not penetrate into the office of the managing director. The remoteness of his room was necessary also in that at one time the cars of the managing director, the sub-manager, the mill superintendent, and the secretary had been left near the opening of his funnel and had become sprinkled with gold.

Beside him as he worked were two bottles of milk. 'It washes the paint off me lungs,' he explained. 'They gotta give me a quart a day by law.'

He took a long draught from one of the bottles, then suddenly began coughing. The handkerchief that he drew from his mouth contained spittle of gold.

'It washes the paint off me lungs,' he explained.

Upon the end of her nose was a small, bluish, black spot slightly sunken. She often touched it with her finger and looked at it in the mirror.

She was fifty-three years old.

She earned her living by piece-work, picking tacking threads from silk shirts and pyjamas for a Brunswick factory. They gave her their best and most expensive work because she was so careful.

She worked in her kitchen spreading the shirts out upon the table and bending over them almost reverently. Some of the shirts were sold for thirty shillings. She worked till eleven o'clock at night so that the factory could pick up the completed articles first thing each morning.

The work was a strain on the eyes and made her very tired. She must have glasses. She went to a doctor. He said, 'What is that mark on your nose?' She didn't know. He looked at it through a glass. 'You will have to visit the hospital regularly and get this attended to,' he said. 'You will have to have radium.'

She was afraid and said, 'Will it cost much?'

'How much are you earning?' he asked.

'Seven and sixpence a week,' she replied. 'I get a penny ha'penny a dozen for picking threads from silk shirts and pyjamas.'

An Edge Setter is a machine that beats the edges of soles into shape.

Operating it is heavy work. The shoe is held tightly against a vibrating piece of steel while every muscle and nerve in the operator's arms shakes in a frenzy of movement. It has turned men into nervous wrecks.

In 1927 the labour cost of a pair of shoes was 3s 10d; in 1933 it was 2s. In the speed-up factories today men are driven to make this figure even lower.

For every minute of the eight and three-quarter hour day an edge setter operator stands before his machine he puts through one pair of shoes.

But a man can put through more when he begins in the morning and just after his lunch, so more is expected of him at these times.

At five o'clock, his arms still twitching, he is released, too tired to read, too tired to talk much, and besides there is 525 pair to be put through tomorrow.

Seagulls live on food thrown over from ships. They seize the scraps tossed away by the cooks and haunt the boats awaiting cargo.

Sometimes a bucket is lowered over the side of the ship when it is at the wharf and the seagulls gather round and eat from the bucket. They get to know the man who feeds them and early in the morning they wait in groups for him to appear at the ship's edge.

The cold wind and rain from the sea often drive them inland, but food is scarce there and they return to the wharves again.

Where they sleep at nights is a mystery. It is cold by the sea in the winter time and they must have shelter. Some can be seen huddled in bags sleeping beneath sheds. It is not of birds I speak, but of the men who live on the wharves and subsist by grace of the kindness of ships' cooks. They call them seagulls.

AUSTRALIAN PICTURE-BOOK II

'I TOOK the rap for a fiver,' he said. 'I was fined five bob the first time, but I've been up seventeen times since then.'

With the camera to his eye he kept taking photos and handing out cards as he talked.

'I suppose the firm you work for pays your fines,' I said.

'Not on your life they don't,' he said. 'I take the knock every time I go up.'

'Taking photos in the street doesn't seem much of a crime,' I said.

'It's against the law,' he replied.

'Why do you still do it?'

'A bloke's gotta live,' he said.

They rush forward with old bags and cram the decaying fruit and vegetables, the outer leaves of cabbages, into the gaping mouths.

The sacks are soon full and bulge like bloated bodies. They raise them on their backs and stagger to billy carts or to frail wagons attached to old ponies. They come back for more. Sometimes they get many sacks of discarded fruit and vegetables from the pit at the Victoria Market.

These old men, decayed like the fruit they scramble for, sell their bulging bags to the cheap cafes whose patrons are too poor to pay more than sixpence for a three-course meal.

London, 25 November—The late Mr Harry Bellingham Howard Smith, shipping director, who died in Australia, left estate in England and the Commonwealth valued at £1,077,012 — *News Item.*

From the bowels of the tourist ships the firemen can sometimes hear the laughter of the passengers and the slip, slip of their feet dancing on the deck above them.

Each passenger pays £35 for a trip round the islands. The firemen are paid £2 per week.

For four hours at a time they stand half naked before roaring furnaces shovelling in the coal that drives the mighty engines. The sweat that's wrung from out their blackened bodies leaves streaks of cleanness on their hides.

From where they work the firemen can sometimes hear the laughter of the passengers and the slip, slip of their dancing on the deck above them.

She worked in the factory, but she was sweeping out the office when she fainted. We all stood up. She was huddled on the floor. She looked so very small. Yet she must have been fourteen.

We lifted her on to the table — she was very light — and stood round her anxiously while the typist bathed her face with water.

She sat up and looked about her. She was confused. I said, 'Do you feel better now?' She said, 'Yes.'

We made her a cup of tea. When she was drinking the tea I questioned her. She answered me very softly. It was hard to hear her above the roar of the factory.

She told me that she hadn't had any breakfast. It appeared she always went without breakfast. There were eight in the family. She was the eldest and the only one working. They depended on her wages for the food they ate.

She was earning fourteen and six a week.

Four of them stood watching. One was very young. His trousers were patched at the knees. The other three were old men.

They leant in silence against the brick wall of the alley. They were watching a door.

Beside the door were two garbage tins. They were old

tins, battered and very dirty. One leaked sluggishly.

Sometimes a wind moved down the alley. When it eddied and passed the men it brought to them the putrid smell of the tins beside the door. It also carried with it the honk of cars flashing past the alley's mouth.

At a quarter past six the door opened. The four men moved forward. A man appeared carrying a bucket. He emptied its contents into one of the garbage tins. He tapped the upturned bucket against the edge of the tin so that none of its contents would remain adhered to the sides. He returned through the door and closed it behind him.

The four men gathered round the garbage tin like vultures round a carcass. They dipped with their hands, bending and rising, bending and rising. They gave each handful they raised a cursory examination.

The alley was at the rear of a hotel in the heart of Melbourne. The food they ate was the discarded remnants of the counter lunches—the crusts and meat scraps disdained by the hotel's belching patrons.

RATTLY BOB

ONE of his testicles had been removed. The scrotum was partly eaten away. When coughing he made a rattling sound the result of the gradual destruction of his lungs. The partition between his nostrils had also gone.

They called him Rattly Bob. He was fifty years old.

He was not pleasant to look at and the management of the Western Australian arsenic plant in which he worked were not anxious that he be seen.

The ore in this particular district contains the gold in arsenical pyrites. When treated in the plant to extract the gold, the arsenic becomes volatile and goes straight from the solid into the gaseous state from where it can be precipitated by any coolness.

Formerly it was precipitated in large chambers which baffled and cooled it. But the loss from the three hundred foot smoke stack was enormous and the wind-borne particles of arsenic polluted the countryside, killing insects and animals; and cattle twenty miles away died from the poisonous crystals dropping in their troughs.

So they improved the plant.

Yet there was still an absence of ants, flies, caterpillars, birds, dogs, cats and cows within a radius of a mile to a mile and a half from the works.

In the mornings the ground had a light, white covering of arsenic precipitated by the cool night air. Rain water was undrinkable, the arsenic-sprinkled iron roofs having poisoned the supply. The swimming pool had to be roofed.

Dogs walking on the deadly ground contracted sores, licked their paws and died.

Only men could live there—men who would one day be like Rattly Bob.

So further improvements were made and two years ago Electrical Precipitators at a cost of £100,000 were installed and the loss from the stacks was reduced.

Flies can now live half a mile from the plant and dogs can gaze at it from unpolluted fields a mile away.

But the men working there still have to wear silk bloomers beneath their trousers to prevent the arsenic dust filtering through their clothes and starting up irritation in the damp places of the body, leading to arsenic dermatitis. And men still become ill and leave and sometimes return, finding a need of arsenic in their ruined systems. And others still wait to take the place of those who with health undermined, are forced to quit.

But Rattly Bob does not quit. Rattly Bob can't quit. Rattly Bob is good for nothing else. Hideous scars in armpit and groin are the rewards of his labour. His lungs still rattle when he coughs. The hundred thousand pound Precipitators did not cure the rattle of his lungs. The hundred thousand pound Precipitators did not make him a man again. Yet he still works on. Where dogs and cats fester and die, he still works on . . .

Rattly Bob—a half man—an employee of a Western Australian arsenic plant.

TOMORROW

LAST Sunday night I stood in front of the Argus buildings waiting for two friends. We were going to a New Theatre performance. It was cold. A wind came round the corner. I thrust my hands into the pockets of my overcoat and crouched against the wall. Hell! It's cold for February, I thought. I couldn't get over how cold it was.

My friends were late. A man lurched round the corner. He was drunk. I looked at his face and saw that he was an Aborigine. He stood before me, one arm outstretched in an effort to place his hand upon my shoulder. He swayed and his hand retreated from me. He came forward and his arm slid past my cheek and draped itself round my shoulders.

''s'all right, boy; 's'all right,' he said.

'It's all right with me, too,' I said.

He was very tall and had to bend to bring his face near mine. He wore a very old and tattered overcoat. It had been grey, once. His head drooped and hung loosely from the neck. His dull gaze was directed at the pavement.

'I'm a tramp,' he said. 'All blacks are tramps.'

I thought about this. 'Yes, things are tough,' I said, almost to myself.

He raised his head and looked into my eyes. I could see the deep lines in his cheeks.

'I can't help you, boy,' he said sadly. 'I got nothin'. I got nothin' at all.'

'That's all right,' I said. 'I'm jake.'

'I know where you can get a bed,' he said, almost eagerly. 'Do you want a bed?'

So as not to impress upon him too cruelly the difference in our circumstances and so that I might still preserve the nature of the contact between us, I answered, 'Yes. I do want a bed.'

He was pleased. 'Look,' he said. 'You go up past the Melbourne Hospital. There's a church place up there. They'll give you a bed. Now, look. You go up past the Melbourne Hospital. Now, look. You'll get a bed. I know about them.'

'Thank's ever so much,' I said. 'I'll go there. But what about you? Have you got a bed?'

'I'm all right,' he said, swaying a little. 'I had a bob. I got a bed first. I went out after I had got a bed. I had a bob, see. I'm right.'

He became cheerful at the thought of the bed he had paid for.

'I'm right,' he said.

'But what about tomorrow?' I asked.

The import of the words slowly penetrated his mind.

He became very still. His swaying stopped. But what about tomorrow? His arm dropped from my shoulders.

'Yess . . . tomorrow,' he said abstractedly, 'Tomorrow . . .'

His cheerfulness had gone. He suddenly appeared very old and helpless. He drew a breath, and turned, and walked clumsily away from me, his shoulders sagging.

When he had staggered a little way he stopped and turning, said vaguely, 'Tomorrow, eh! Yes. Yes, go up there, boy. You'll get a bed. Yes, that's right. Tomorrow . . .'

'WE'RE BEGINNING TO THINK, NOW'

THEY were sitting on their swags by the side of the road. The dust of cars sometimes obscured them in a gust of foul breath. I was doing about thirty. As I passed, one gestured with a closed hand and projecting thumb. He did it mechanically as if expecting no response. He hardly looked at me. He just gestured as if from habit.

My brakes are bad. I went for about fifty yards before I could pull up. I looked back through the rear glass and saw one of them jump to his feet and stand watching me. He grabbed a swag and spoke rapidly to his companion. They came running towards me, their black billies dangling from their hands.

They confronted me rather awkwardly as if doubting my intention to give them a lift. 'Hop in,' I said, and their faces cleared and they smiled at me.

They smelt of sweat. Dust had caked their lips and eyelids. They were tired and foot-sore. They had walked from Sydney, they said.

We got talking. One of them had a cauliflower ear. He had fought in different boxing troupes and told me of his experiences.

'I got ten bob a fight in one troupe,' he said. 'I used to average about four fights a week, but once in Maryborough I had five fights in the one day. Hell! I was bad after that. I was crook for a fortnight.'

He told me that in another troupe they got seven and sixpence a fight but were supplied with plenty of plonk.

The other chap had been in a buck-jump show. He had been paid seven and six a night, but had to give it up because of a kick on the head from one of the horses. He was always getting headaches.

We pulled up and had a feed under a bridge. I had some tucker on board. They were great chaps. We sat round the fire yarning.

'I've been on the road since I was fifteen,' said the boxer. 'Many's the time I've slept under this bridge. There's a big house on the left, up a little way from here.'

'I saw it,' I said.

'A bloke gave me a pair of trousers there once. I had them for years. Hell, they was good pants.'

The other chap told me that he had lost his job when he turned twenty-one.

'I was workin' in a flock factory,' he said. 'When I got the bullet I set off for Sydney. An Italian gave me a lift in an International truck. He was a white man.'

'I met a bloke like that once,' said the boxer. 'He'd do anything for you.'

'You know when I had a job I was contented,' said his companion. 'I went out with my girl at nights and I never used to think much. But after I got out on the roads I began to think. When you are out of work and hungry, that's the time when you begin to think.'

'I'll say it is,' said the boxer.

'I used to think that the job was all that mattered,' said the other. 'But I can see different, now. Coves like us will always be out of work until we own all the factories and can work for the good of all of us. Why should Mick and me be tramping the roads when there are people howling out for boots and clothes that we could help to make for them.'

'That day is coming,' I said.

'Yes. It is that,' said the boxer. 'We're beginning to think now.'

IT WON'T ALWAYS BE SO

HE WAS one of a bunch of prisoners who, having pleaded guilty to various offences, was waiting in the cells below the Court room before being called up for sentence.

His father had appeared to plead for him.

When his son stepped into the dock they looked at each other with a quick glance of affection.

The son, about twenty-three, pale, with a face upon which worry had planted a strained, defiant look.

The father coughed often. His face was a more matured and shrunken replica of his son's. He wore a returned soldier's badge.

'Have you anything to say?' asked the judge, looking at the boy. The prisoner glanced quickly at his father.

The Clerk of Courts rose and whispered to the judge. He pointed towards the older man. The judge nodded and spoke to the father.

'Mr Robins, I believe you want to say something. Would you take your place in the witness stand please?'

The father mounted the stand and after being sworn in began to speak.

'Your honour, I was wondering if my boy could be released on bond. It's this way. I haven't been able to work since the war. I was gassed and wounded bad. This lad was thrown out of work in the worst of the depression. He was put off when he was twenty-one. They had to pay him more, you see. He has been out of work ever since. He has never given me any trouble.'

The father put his hand over his mouth and through the court there sounded the articulate gift of Flander's gas. His frail body shook with his coughing.

'He's a good son,' he went on at last. 'But he couldn't get work anywhere. But last week a bloke I know got him a job. That's if he can start next week. It's the first chance he's had, and on account of me only getting a war pension, we find it hard to keep going. If I hadn't been so badly wounded I could have got work. The gas isn't as bad as my side. But if you could let him out on bond everything would be right. This is the first chance he has had to get a job.'

'Where is this position available?' asked the judge.

'In the Maribyrnong Munition factory,' said the father.

GUNS FOR CHILDREN

IT HAPPENED in Bourke Street during Christmas week.* The street was full of people: tired mothers dragging children by their strained, extended arms; men laden with parcels; penniless men standing ignored at the kerb side, their hands thrust into empty pockets.

The red facade of one shop might appropriately have been coloured with blood. Its window was an arsenal. An arsenal for children who could view in safety miniature replicas of the weapons that may some day blast their bodies asunder.

Within the window stood a junior sales girl. Her face was expressionless; her movements were mechanical. She turned the handle of a toy machine gun. Sparks spluttered from its mouth and bounced on the glass of the window. On the leg of the machine gun was the caption 'Made in Japan'.

Encircling the girl was a miniature roadway of steel. Tiny tanks spiked with guns plodded their way around it. They rocked their way over the obstacles placed there to demonstrate the possibilities of their caterpillar wheels. Armoured cars, much swifter, raced past them. Toy soldiers of lead guarded the roadway. One had fallen down and lay athwart the track.

The armoured cars and tanks bumped over him as they passed. His body quivered at the impact of each speeding vehicle. Gradually the paint wore off his face and it became a grey colour like the face of a corpse. A corpse made in Japan.

* 1937.

So that the people before the window might be kept interested, the girl had to be continually winding the armoured cars and the tanks. She held the toys in her hand to wind them. She then placed them on the track again and they would shoot away from beneath her hand like frightened things. When she was winding the toys the machine gun was silent. It stood there pointing at the people: at the women and children among the people, in silent menace.

Above the girl's head, suspended by long cotton threads, were many aeroplanes. Every now and then she jigged or struck the threads that held them. They jerked into life at her touch and dived and swooped so swiftly that it became difficult to read the names painted on their sides: Bomber, Fighter, Transport plane. Through the windows of the largest one could be seen the tiny heads of little men. They had military caps upon their hollow heads.

Their heads contained nothing at all whatsoever. How their plane flew. It shot to the top of its pendulum swing, turned, swooped low over the head of the little sales girl as if dropping bombs upon her and sped away again before returning in another dive.

The aeroplanes were made in Japan, too.

It was very hard to get near the window to see all this. The people were crowded so thickly round the glass. But even from the kerb one could hear the splutter of the machine gun, the b-r-r of its mechanism.

It was so loud that the one-legged digger leaning on his crutches at the kerb's edge stopped his singing and looked disconsolately into the hat he held in his hand. It contained three pennies.

He took a deep breath and started again: 'O, give me a home, where the buffalo roam . . .'

B-r-r-r-r-r went the machine gun.

THE DARK PEOPLE

TO THE east of Darwin lie the vast swamp lands that skirt the western boundary of Arnhem Land. Here, in the wet season, the long grass is flattened by the rain and wind so that it lies upon the water like the drenched hair of an animal. Criss-crossing this enormous expanse of green are the uncovered waterways made by the buffalo pushing a pathway for themselves across the flood plains.

Here the magpie geese rise in their thousands, the wind of their wings disturbing the tranquillity of the open pools that dot the swamps.

Beyond these swamps rise the ramparts of Arnhem Land. Sandstone cliffs, carved by the wind and rain of centuries into fantastic pillars and tottering walls, stand with their base hidden in a screen of boulders and shattered stone.

These cliffs guard Australia's largest native reserve, the · last untouched home of the black.

Arnhem Land, which stretches beyond these cliffs to the waters of the Gulf of Carpentaria, is not an hospitable region where the black man can live in comfort, where game is plentiful and vegetable food abundant. Rather is it a hard and forbidding land that breeds a strong and independent and courageous people.

These are the qualities that mark the blacks who roam its bush or build their mia-mias along its coast. It was these people who resisted the white man's advance long after those in other areas had been vanquished.

There are probably no more than four thousand blacks in

Arnhem Land today. Most of them live on the missions that are established on its northern coastline. Odd family groups still live the nomadic life of their ancestors, but the lure of the white man's food and tobacco is strong and they make periodical visits to the missions to replenish their supply.

One such family group came striding in from the bush as I sat beneath a tamarind tree at one of these centres. They marched in single file, led by a tall native carrying four stone-headed spears and a woomera. Transfixed on one of the spears was a goanna. The leader strode with an erect carriage and there was pride in the lift of his head.

Behind him walked two other men with a dead wallaby hanging from a pole resting on their shoulders. They were also armed with spears. One of them had a huge parrot fish strung on to his woomera.

Then came four women, two of whom had babies riding on their shoulders. The babies clung to their mothers' hair, their chubby hands buried deep in the black, wavy locks. Each woman carried a dilly-bag suspended from a string that passed around her forehead. The bags rested between their shoulders. They were laden with water-lily roots, yams and the nuts of the zamia palm.

Walking steadily in the rear were the children—nine of them. One little girl of about eight carried a baby sister on her shoulder. She kept her eyes on the ground as if the baby's weight made it necessary for her to place her feet with greater care.

All the children had thin legs, the thighs being almost as slender as the calves. Their bellies were tight and rounded and seemed out of proportion to the frailty of their limbs. They had happy, smiling faces and dark brown eyes shaded by long lashes. Their teeth were white and even and flashed between their full lips when they laughed.

The party gathered round the mia-mia of a tribal relative. The men laid their spears upon the ground and squatted beside them while they talked to the resident blacks who had watched their approach and who had selected this spot for a confab.

The mothers had seated themselves and were feeding the

babies. I had walked over to the mia-mia to have a look at these babies. They were a dark coffee-brown in colour, though the palms of their hands and the soles of their feet were almost white. Their skin seemed to have a bloom on it as if they were still untouched by wind and rain.

One of them, a little girl, lay cradled in her mother's arms sucking contentedly. But a bauhinia blossom on the bush beneath which her mother sat claimed her attention. She stopped the quick movements of her lips and lay looking up at it with an absorbed expression upon her face, the nipple of her mother's breast idle between her parted lips.

Her mother gazed down on her, a gentle smile on her face. She touched the baby's cheek with a dark finger, then looked up at the flower. She raised her arm and plucked the blossom, which she waved before her baby's eyes in a playful gesture. The baby smiled, then began sucking again.

The blacks are devoted to their children and though they spoil them outrageously the children are thoughtful and kind.

It is interesting to compare those factors that condition the lives of the piccaninnies with those that condition the lives of white children. In the beginning there is no difference between the children of both races except in colour. Black babies and white babies show the same interest in their little hands, which they hold in front of their faces as they lie relaxed on a bed or on sand. They waggle their fingers and crow. They make purposeless movements with their legs and jerk their arms and look steadily at their mother's face while she gives them the breast.

When they begin walking they toddle uncertainly on vague journeys of exploration and examine leaves and twigs with a similar interest.

The change comes when they are old enough to play with other children. Now the non-competitive nature of the blacks' civilisation gives a joyous quality to the games of the piccaninnies, a quality that is not manifest in the playgrounds of the white.

A babble of sound comes from the school playgrounds of white children. There are shouting, high cries and laughter, but there are also protests, demands, recriminations. In its total effect it is not a happy sound.

How different when one listens to a group of black children at play. They play with singing cries, with joyful notes, with laughter. They are like a flock of birds chattering in the grass.

The reason for the difference in the attitude of the black child and the white child towards their playmates is this: the piccaninnies play with things that are available to them all. Their toys are rush spears, stones, shells, sticks and coloured clays. Possessiveness in these things just doesn't exist. If one child has a rush spear, the other child can pick one too. If shells are suddenly found interesting, all the children run down to the beach and get shells.

No one envies what the other has since no one possesses what the other can't have also.

The toys of white children are not so easily obtained, and those who have them are the envy of those who haven't—thus the arguments on their playgrounds.

I sat one day and watched a black boy of ten called Bandarawoi organise a spear fight. Bandarawoi was thin even by blackfellow standards. His legs were like sticks, but when he ran they carried him with speed and grace.

I found it easy to make this boy laugh and since his laughter was contagious his companions always seemed to be in a state of merriment. They referred to him as a 'funny fella'.

'He funny fella,' they would say, looking at him when he was convulsed with laughter, as if such a capacity for enjoyment were not quite normal.

And, indeed, his laughter at times did seem too powerful an expression of the joy he felt in watching me poke faces, act the clown or simulate fear. He always bent forward from the hips when laughing so that his head was brought on to the same level as his knees. But there were times when even this posture was incapable of supporting the immensity of his mirth and then he would stagger to a tree and embrace it or lie on the ground and roll till his laughter had ceased.

He liked games in which he could leap and yell, so mock

fights with rush spears was a favourite of his. He divided the children, boys and girls, into two sides. The spears were rushes and they threw them at each other with great skill.

Bandarawoi led his yelling warriors in charges or crept with them through the long grass to escape an ambush or a foray. Happy cries punctuated the game. There was continual laughter. Only rarely do black children lose their tempers, but when they do it is an undisciplined outburst that quickly burns out.

One little boy, 'speared' a number of times without being able to retaliate as skilfully, threw himself on the ground in a rage. He kicked himself round in circles as he lay on his back on the sand. Bandarawoi gave one glance at him, then led the children away to continue the game where his screams would not interrupt them.

In a little while the boy sat up, incapable of persevering in such a convincing display of temper when there was no one there to witness it. When he rejoined his companions he was smiling again and they, in their turn, made no reference to his outburst but played with him as before.

Bandarawoi's skill with a rush spear impressed me and I asked him would he teach me to throw one. He evidently thought a toy spear was too undignified a weapon for this purpose, so he raced away to his father's mia-mia and after a hurried consultation with that agreeable man he returned with a full-sized spear and woomera.

Three of his small companions joined him in giving me this lesson.

'Hold it allasame dis way now.'

I held it. I did all he said. I fitted the hook at the end of the woomera into the notch at the end of the spear. I poised, then threw.

The spear buried its barbs in the earth a short distance away, quivered a moment, then sank slowly to the earth. It was a humiliating cast, but the children acclaimed it as a tremendous throw.

'Good shot, Gurrawilla,' they cried. 'Number one shot.'

They called me 'Gurrawilla', which means 'song-maker' and is the nearest word they could get to 'writer'.

'Good shot. Number one shot.'

Such was their praise that I changed my opinion about my throw and felt rather pleased with myself. I wondered how I compared with these boys in throwing a spear.

'Now you throw,' I said. 'Let me see how far you can throw it.'

But they didn't greet my request with much enthusiasm.

'Nudder time,' they said. 'You too good. You number one.'

But I insisted, so rather reluctantly they lined up and, one by one, cast the spear in a demonstration of their skill. Each one set his jaw, ran a few steps forward, then hurled the spear with every evidence of a set determination to beat me. But each throw fell short of mine.

I was surprised and pleased and as I made my way back to the mission house I concluded, with some enthusiasm, that maybe I was a natural spear-thrower with a gift that was being lost to the world of sport.

When I reached my room I looked out of the window and, down on the beach, I saw Bandarawoi and his companions competing against each other in throwing the spear. Each boy threw the spear at least four times as far as I had done. These children of the blackfellow had a rare thoughtfulness. They allowed a man of a different colour to themselves to win at a game at which they excelled, merely to please him.

The ambition of all the little black boys is to be a good hunter, but the lives led by the little girls is a preparation for motherhood and gatherers of food. They are devoted to their smaller sisters and brothers and, when called from play to look after the baby, as they so often are, they never go reluctantly but run to their mother almost with eagerness. They carry the babies on their shoulders as their mothers do, and sometimes one feels that the plump piccaninnies sitting so placidly with their creased legs round the necks of their sisters, would exhaust them with their weight.

I was once at a mission that was being visited by a doctor. The doctor entered an old dilapidated galvanised-iron hut to examine a child suspected of having tuberculosis, common amongst the blacks. The child must have been terrified at his entry. She cried loudly in her fear.

Children, fascinated by her cries, gathered round the hut in a frightened group and peered through cracks in the wall. They did not speak to each other, but when a cry stronger than the rest came from the child within the hut, they glanced at each other with frightened, questioning eyes and the little ones clutched the skirts of older sisters. On the outskirts of the group a little girl stood holding the hand of a baby brother who had not long taken his first steps. She suddenly released her brother's hand and moved closer to the hut. He watched her, feeling afraid at the responsibility of standing alone without a comforting hand to grasp. Sometimes the cry from within the hut was too terrifying to be borne and all the children moved in a sudden panic back from the hut, looking at it over their shoulders as if it had menaced them. When this happened the baby brother didn't move but looked nervously from face to face, then back at his sister, as if searching for enlightenment.

Then the doctor emerged. The children scattered, running desperately for the shelter of trees. With them went the little boy's sister who, in her panic, had forgotten her brother. The baby brother, seeing her go, yelled in fear. The sister heard him and turned. She had a moment of indecision, then raced back towards him, her thin legs twinkling. She did not look at him as she ran, but kept her desperate eyes on the doctor. The little boy awaited her coming with uplifted arms, his yells even louder.

When she reached him she spread her legs wide apart and, with a struggle, lifted him so that his chest rested on her clasped hands. She staggered away with him, trying to run but unable to do so because of his weight. When she reached the mango trees she stopped, panting, and looked back, but she still held him tightly. He had stopped crying. His arms were around her neck and he looked back too.

From early childhood the girls are trained for their future task of food gatherers. It is the responsibility of the native women to keep their men folk supplied with vegetable food, referred to contemptuously by the men as 'woman tucker'. Each day the mothers, with babies astride their necks, go walking through the bush in search of yams, edible roots and fruits from the bush trees. With them go the little girls whose task it is to help their mothers fill the dilly-bags the mothers carry on their backs. Many bush yams are poisonous and the girls must learn to recognise these. Other roots must be pounded and washed or soaked for days before they are fit to eat. The mothers explain these things to their daughters as they walk through the bush.

Once when accompanying a group of women and children on their daily hunt for 'woman tucker' I dug up a large yam I had discovered and handed it to a little girl to take to her mother. She looked at it, then tossed it aside.

'Him cheeky,' she said, her way of saying that the yam was poisonous.

The children chew the stems of grass as they walk, the juice evidently supplying them with a needed food. When they come to a 'wild grape' vine they crowd around it like birds plucking the grapes and popping them into their mouths with great eagerness.

The babies seem to eat anything. Sometimes when a mother comes to a spot where yams are plentiful she lifts her baby from her shoulders and places him on the ground. On such occasions, his expression suggests he has been placed in the midst of an abundant food supply. He reaches out eagerly, seizing twigs and pebbles and pieces of bark. Each find is thrust into his mouth for a quick chew before it is discarded. But sometimes a grub or a caterpillar or a beetle comes his way and these he swallows with excitement as if he is savouring a rare and delightful flavour that is generally denied him. Only recently my baby daughter ate a caterpillar she had found in the grass. Judging by her expression, I am sure she enjoyed it.

Babies are the same the world over, it seems. Given equal opportunities this similarity could continue into their adult years and then the black man and the white could really live as brothers.

I WONDER WHAT HE THINKS ABOUT?

OLD Ummarangun squatted on the sand with his thin arms
wound round his legs so that his chin rested on his knees.
Beside him lay his spears and his woomera. The sun was
setting across the bay and he was absorbed in the convoluted
clouds that towered like flaming mountains above the sea.

I thought I would find him there. He often sat watching
the sunset. He had a habit of sitting for long periods looking
at the hills or at the melaleuca trees that followed the river.
When the scene before him had an arresting beauty, memories
enveloped him and gave to his expression some quality of
poignancy.

He was not an old man, though the Macassar beard that
adorned his chin was white and the lines that crossed his
forehead were those that come with the experiences of years.

He had been a famous song-man in the Cape Stewart tribe,
it was said. But that was before a battalion of A.I.F. boys had
cleared a patch of bushland in his country and members of
his tribe had learnt to work for the white soldiers.

He had never demeaned himself by working for the white
man. He had always stood aloof, his dignified bearing and
inflexible reserve a reproach to those of his people who gave
up their freedom for the sake of tobacco and ready-made
food.

He had not responded to the many advances I made to
gain his friendship, though he treated me with respect.

I wished that I knew more about him. His aloofness was a
challenge, and his preoccupation with those things in which

any appeal they possessed could only be aesthetic was intriguing and suggested a mind that responded to beauty.

Once I saw him pick an hibiscus flower and stand gazing at it, his limbs rigid and still. Blackfellows did not ordinarily pick flowers.

Sergeant Cooper thought he was mad.

'Who wouldn't be in this forsaken stretch of coast?' he said. 'In the future I'll be satisfied to read about Northern Australia in the pages of a book. I've had this camp. I'll be going like old Ummarangun if I have to stop here much longer.'

The sergeant thought all blacks were a bit queer. I often sat in his hut and talked to him about the natives.

'They are only concerned with what they eat,' he said one night. 'A blackfellow has no sense of beauty. There is no word in their language for beauty.'

'How do you know?' I asked him.

'I asked one of them.'

'Maybe he didn't know what you meant.'

'Maybe he didn't—too thick in the head.'

'I'm sure they have a word for beauty,' I said stubbornly.

'I'll bet you a quid they haven't,' he argued. 'You'd like to think they had a word for beauty. If they haven't, all your arguments for the past fortnight mean nothing. I've watched you. You won't face up to facts. Next thing you'll be arguing that a blackfellow is as good as a white man.'

'I like old Ummarangun,' I said defensively. 'Have you seen the design on his woomera? He couldn't have carved it unless he had an appreciation of beauty in design—and intelligence, too.'

'Oh, that argument!' exclaimed the sergeant contemptuously. 'Away back, some black has cut strokes along the grain and knots in a piece of wood used as a woomera. Others have copied it because of this chap's success in hunting. Gradually it got altered into the pattern old Ummarangun carves on his woomera today.'

'Next time I see old Ummarangun I'll ask him if there is a word in his language for beauty,' I said. 'A word that means being stirred by some object or scene. He'll know. He's always watching sunsets.'

'You know why he watches sunsets?' asked the sergeant, thrusting his head towards me.

'I think I do,' I replied.

'Well, you are wrong,' said the sergeant. 'He's gone queer and he imagines his daughter will come back at sunset. Anyway, whatever he thinks, it has something to do with his daughter.'

'His daughter!' I exclaimed. 'You have never told me anything about a daughter.'

'Didn't I? I thought you knew. Everyone in the camp knows the story.'

'What is it?'

'When we first came up here old Ummarangun had a daughter. She would be about eight, I suppose. She used to run a lot and jump about and laugh. She was always walking a step behind him.

'I think her mother was dead. If she wasn't, some bush black must have pinched her from Ummarangun. Anyway, the old chap thought a lot of this kid. She used to dart in when any of us tossed a butt away, then she would race away and give it to her dad. I don't think she ever missed a butt.

'She had thin legs and used to look up at you, grinning, when you spoke to her—a kid like that.'

'I wish I could meet her,' I said.

'You can't. She's dead,' said the sergeant.

'What happened to her?'

'One evening, about sunset, old Ummarangun was standing waist-deep out on the sand bar spearing fish. The kid was standing in the water about fifty yards away. He had his back to her for a few minutes. When he turned round again she was gone. They reckon a croc got her—there are a lot of them round here.

'He took to sitting on the beach at sunset. In the daytime he'd wander round looking at the ground or at the trees. He carried shells around with him. The kid used to play with shells.'

The sergeant stared at the floor for a few moments, then murmured as if to himself, 'Mad, mad, mad . . . It's funny . . . I wonder what he thinks about! I wonder how he feels!'

He stirred himself at last and looked up at me. 'You won't get much out of old Ummarangun. He's not at home. He'll look at you, that's all.'

Perhaps not, I thought, as I descended the sandhill that skirted the beach and walked towards this old black the white man said was mad. But I could try. Maybe he wasn't as mad as they thought. Maybe he would talk to me.

I sat beside him upon the broken shells that marked the limits of the tide. He did not move, but remained absorbed in the screen of tempestuous colour that stained the sea a dull crimson.

'Hullo, Ummarangun,' I said.

He turned his head and looked at me for a moment, then resumed his contemplation of the low sky.

'Here, have a cigarette,' I said, holding mine towards him.

He took one without speaking, looked at it intently, then placed it behind his ear.

I lit up and smoked in silence. He seemed unconscious of my presence. I picked up his woomera and began examining the design grooved on its surface.

'Did you carve this, Ummarangun?' I asked.

He looked at the woomera abstractedly, his thoughts resisting the attempt of his will to apply them to the throwing stick in my hands.

'Yo,' (yes) he said at last.

'See these curving lines, Ummarangun,' I said, as I followed them round with my finger. 'They are mainmuk (good). But they are more better than mainmuk. We call them "beautiful". Have you a word that means beautiful — more better than mainmuk — yindi mainmuk (big good)?'

He was listening intently now. His eyes had lost their pre-occupied expression and were registering the movements of my hand with understanding.

I waited for him to reply, but he looked at me questioningly and I continued.

'When you see these things that are more better than mainmuk your heart beats quickly.' I placed my hands upon his chest, the ridged cicatrices that scarred it, hard beneath my palm.

64

'Your heart inside there,' I said. 'It beats thump, thump. You look at this thing long time. Ah! this is a very mainmuk thing. I feel more better. I am singing inside me.

'That sunset . . . See . . .' and I pointed across the bay. 'It is the word. It is a singing thing.'

He looked at the sunset, his eyes clouding to some troubling memory that sought, for a moment, to occupy his mind. He touched his closed eyes with his fingers, then grunted and looked at me again.

'Some women have it,' I continued. 'It is in their face. All men who see it say, "She is beautiful—she is more better than mainmuk."

'It is in dancing; in a voice, sometimes. When some people speak to you the sound is yindi mainmuk. It makes your skin go funny. Just like sand being poured on your skin—like that.'

He smiled and nodded.

'Without these things the world no good—dark, empty,' I went on. 'Better we die if no things like this are here. The word means those things that make us feel mainmuk. We call it "beauty". Tell me your word for this thing.'

He suddenly leant towards me, smiling in some strange, tremulous fashion, and said, 'Marakari.'

'Marakari! Is that the word?'

'Yo.'

'Does it make your heart beat quickly?'

'Yo.'

'Is it in the sunset there?'

'Yo.'

'In flowers, and birds and trees?'

'Yo.'

'It means the thing that makes you feel a singing inside of you?'

'Yo.'

'Marakari!' I said softly. 'So that is the word.'

'Well,' I said to the sergeant that night, 'the blacks have a word for "beauty" after all. Old Ummarangun told me. How do you like your eggs done?'

He grinned. 'He's pulling your leg. What word did he say?'

'Marakari.'

'Marakari, be blowed! That was the name of old Ummarangun's little daughter.'

THE UNITING ONES

LONG ago, in the days before the white man came to Australia, indeed in those days long before any human being had come to this country, it was a land of birds and animals and trees. In those days there were no boundaries between countries. The food, the climate, the vegetation of all sections of the world were available to those who visited them. Birds were the great travellers. They could roam the world, and many did. It was the time of no wars, the time of peace; birds knew nothing of war; they were carriers of peace and friendship.

I was travelling across Mongolia in a rattling train that clanked its way across wide plains and by rolling hills that seemed to me to be empty of all life. I looked out at the landscape from the window of the train and I thought to myself, 'I am in Mongolia. I've always wanted to visit Mongolia. I must not let one bush, one blade of grass, one tree escape my attention. I must absorb all that I am looking at so that it will remain with me forever, for I will never come to Mongolia again.'

The train was travelling beside a shallow creek that gurgled and splashed its way over stones and rocks, and its banks were lined with shrubs that seemed to me to resemble ti-tree. The creek was a warm and friendly one and I could hear its gurgling as the train followed its course. Beyond this creek was a flat plain about a mile across. On its far side stretched a range of mountains. This mountain range was treeless. It was a mountain range of sharp peaks and precipitous spurs that fell down from the crest of the main range and broadened out into gentle undulations before disappearing into the plain. This mountain range was etched against a duck-egg blue sky, so sharply and so clearly that it looked more like the miniature ranges of mountains made of plasticine that we sometimes see in schools. It stood out against the sky, its crest serrated and cleft with battlements and sharp peaks, and this long crest appeared to be pasted on to the duck-egg blue sky. It was a darker blue than the sky, and appeared two dimensional.

The sun was setting. It lit up the western side of the branching spurs, turning their dark blue colouring into triangles of light. The eastern side of the spurs was in shadow and a darker blue than the rest of the range.

I looked at this sight with wonder. It was so beautiful. Yet it was empty of life. It seemed to me that there should be living things in this landscape, revealing to me something significant about Mongolia.

My interpreter, sitting next to me, noticed my expression and said: 'You are a long way from Australia now, Mr Marshall,' and, indeed, as I looked at this land, I did seem to be a long way from Australia. Australia was far to the south, away down there behind mountains and plains and strange seas.

Then I noticed a flickering flock of black and white appear over the crest of the range and stand out against the sky. It was a flock of birds and they twinkled very quickly from black to white as they veered in their flight. They came swiftly down from the crest of the range, flying over the long spurs and descending lower and lower till they were winging their way over the narrow plain.

They were flying in formation, V formation. There was a leader at the point of the V, and he led them across that plain with strong wing-beats, flying with some urgency I thought, as if they had a long way to go and their time was limited. They came swiftly towards the train and I thrust my head out of the window so that I could watch them. Just before they would have crossed the train they all turned in a simultaneous movement and, for a moment, I could see their long red legs stretching behind them, their long outstretched neck in front of them, the band across their chests, and their powerful beating wings. I recognised them. They were Banded Stilts, birds I had often seen in Australia's summertimes. I waved to them, then turned to my interpreter: 'See those birds up there,' I said with excitement. 'They are Banded Stilts. In a few weeks time they will be winging their way over my home at Eltham. They are on the migratory flight to the south. They will alight in the swamps at Port Melbourne, because I have seen them there. We are not so far from Australia after all. They are symbols. They are uniting my country and your country. How beautiful. How really beautiful!'

MEN OF THE CATTLE COUNTRY

WHERE there are cattle there are men. The herds that string along the stock routes of the north, or wander across the unfenced pastures of the Barkly Tableland, or move restlessly in the yards at the Dajarra railhead, must be watched by men. Men draft them, brand them, pump the water they drink, and, in the end, destroy them.

There are not many of these men—factory workers are far more numerous, there are more men working sheep than cattle—but without them the cities would be starved of beef and Australia would have thousands of square miles of productive country lying useless.

The men who breed the cattle, the station managers and owners, are specialists. It is their job to produce carcasses of export quality, and to do this they must understand the science of breeding. They select their bulls with care, they are constantly culling the cows. They discover the type of beast that thrives best on the country they control. They are constantly trying to improve conditions, to keep down the mortality rate and enlarge their herd.

But to do this they must have labour.

It is sometimes said in the north that any man who goes to work in the Territory is either a tax dodger, a wife starver, a booze artist, or a man who is anxious to avoid becoming a guest of His Majesty.

Maybe the desire to escape the law or the temptation to drink to excess does drive many a man into the lonely places, but there are others who work in solitude by preference.

Of all the jobs that demand the capacity to live alone, that of a 'pumper' is the most unattractive.

On the big stations of the Barkly Tableland the cattle depend, for nine months of the year, on the water drawn from bores. Though windmills are used on government tanks along the stock routes where cattle only water when passing through, they are not used on station tanks where two thousand head of cattle may be watering each day.

A windmill could never pump sufficient water to satisfy the daily thirst of so many. There may be a week or more without wind, long enough for a tank to be emptied and the cattle left without water.

So 'pumpers' are employed, men who live on the tanks and tend the engines that keep the turkey-nest tanks full. These men are not mechanics—any breakdown is repaired by the station engineer—but are generally elderly men who have had to give up more strenuous work or who cannot face up to life amongst their fellows.

When young men take on this job it is generally through ignorance of the conditions they will have to face or because they are 'down and out' and need a cheque to establish themselves again.

I remember driving up to a bore on the Barkly Tableland forty miles from the homestead and seeing a young, unshaven fellow standing beneath a tree rolling his swag as if his very life depended on it. As the truck drew to a stop he yelled at us in a surprisingly loud voice, 'I'm snatching it. I'm shooting through. I've had this job.'

He threw his swag on to the truck almost before it stopped and leaped up after it like a shipwrecked sailor grabbing at a rock.

'Struth!' he exclaimed as he wiped the sweat from his face. 'I thought you was never comin'.'

He had been married down south three months before, he told me, and had only been on the job for a fortnight.

'Why did you come up here?' I asked him.

'The missus and I didn't get on too good,' he said.

The loneliness of these jobs would be intolerable to men who delight in the company of their fellows. As one man said to me, 'The less you like people the easier it is to work on your own.'

One 'pumper', an Englishman newly arrived in this country, asked, with some astonishment, when a bag of flour was being loaded on to the ration truck that was to take him to the bore he had to work, 'What is this for?'

'You'll find out soon enough when you have been out there for a few days,' said one of the ringers standing by.

A fortnight later, when necessity had taught him to make a damper, I saw him at the bore. He looked depressed and commented, as he gazed at an unbroken skyline of grass, 'I've got nothing here for company except a dog and a mouth organ, and I can't play the mouth organ because the dog doesn't like it.'

Yet some men find the life agreeable. One old fellow with a passion for listening to the wireless had three sets in his hut so that if one went 'bung' he could switch on another.

The ration truck called at his hut once a week, stayed a few minutes while the driver unloaded his rations, then moved on across the wide, treeless downs to visit similar huts far beyond the horizon.

You would imagine that these weekly visits would be a welcome break to this old man who lived with only cattle for company. But no; the wireless seemed to supply all his wants.

On one occasion I was on the truck that brought in his weekly rations. The door of his hut was closed as we stopped in front of it. Suddenly the door opened and a head was thrust through the opening.

'Leave them on the ground there,' he yelled, referring to the rations. 'I'm listening to the wireless.'

The door closed again and he disappeared. We unloaded his supplies and went on again. He never even appeared to wave us goodbye.

I remember once, on a remote corner of a run, producing a camera to take a picture of the 'pumper' who had appeared at the door of his hut. He was a distinguished looking man clad in well-laundered shorts and a blue linen shirt.

At the sight of my camera he covered his face with his

hands and sprang backwards into the shadow of his room.

'I'm sorry,' he said in explanation, 'but you know how it is. I am not-er-anxious to be identified.'

I knew how it was, and I put my camera away.

The fugitive, the misfit, the alcoholic, do not survive long in cities. They are moved on or forced to seek places where temptation does not confront them at every turn. You find them in the Territory or round the Gulf Country. Here they find a certain security.

There was 'Whiskers Joe', an alcoholic who, when on a bender, stubbed lighted cigarette butts on his forearm. The smooth scars of old burns dotted his arm from wrist to elbow. He drifted on to the big runs and became a 'pumper'.

And then there was the old fellow who roamed around with one boot on. He had lost the other in a bog and by some strange process of reasoning decided to continue wearing the remaining one. His bare foot had the thick, callous sole of a blackfellow; his booted foot wouldn't turn a burr.

The 'pumper' is rooted to the bore he tends. His work never takes him more than a few yards from his pump.

The drover is a different type. He is a wanderer. Each morning he wakes to a different scene and his eyes become narrowed from gazing over sun-drenched plains. His face has the texture of an old saddle, and his conversation holds you to the campfire when you should be asleep.

'Yes, they go like a flash,' one old drover was telling me, referring to a rush when the sleeping cattle leap to their feet and go thundering off into the night.

'Some camps are worse than others. If you're on drummy ground they'll bust any night. I've seen 'em take off when you throw fat in the fire or bang a tin.'

'It was bad in 1939,' said the horse-tailer who was sitting with us.

'There was some terrible rushes in that year,' agreed the drover. 'Some mobs lost hundreds.'

'I suppose they'd go through anything,' I said.

'They'll do that, too,' said the drover. 'They generally make south in a rush. I pitch the camp to the north of them. Timber won't stop 'em. When they're smashin' through the timber it frightens 'em more. Saplings are going down and cattle are being staked. Then they split. If they split they're hard to stop.'

''Member that night the mob of Barkly cattle bust at the Bottle and Glass camp?' said the horse-tailer.

'Yair,' said the drover. 'I remember it. Bob reckoned I wouldn't hold mine. They lay down all night and never moved.'

'He done his cattle that night,' said the horse-tailer.

'They found some of them thirty miles away,' said the drover.

The drover has other problems besides holding the cattle. After long stretches without water the cattle have to be strung into a bore gradually so that all can drink without interference.

'I held them three miles out,' one drover was telling me, referring to the mob he was taking south. The first water for two days was three miles ahead of them. 'I was frightened of a smash at the bore, but I let a cut go in and held the others till the first lot had a drink. They can smell the water a mile away.'

The terms used by drovers are unfamiliar to city people. I was driving through desert country with a station manager and we came across a drover scouting a mile or two ahead of his mob. He hailed us and we pulled up.

'What's it like ahead?' he asked. 'I'm leading a bad tail.'

'Not too good,' said the manager. 'There's a bit of goose picking a mile ahead, but Harry's been through. He is held up further on with red water.* He's left a tail along the road already. He had a thousand head on this corner and it's well eaten out. If I were you I'd make for the timber a mile on.

'There's horse picking round here, but I need a bit of cattle picking,' said the drover. 'Do you reckon I'll get a couple of drinks at Flannigan's?'

'I think he's pumping on Number 19,' said the manager. 'But you might have a job to get a drink there.'

'I'll have to chance it,' said the drover, then added, 'Harry's got a bad tail, has he?'

* Red water fever is a disease caused by ticks.

'I didn't see them walking,' said the manager, 'but it's a ragtail mob. There's some terrible stuff.'

'I'll pass him tomorrow,' said the drover. 'All I want now is a drink and enough picking to hold them tonight. I better get moving.'

He rode off, swinging loosely to his horse's stride.

The ringers are the stockmen on a station. The cattle pass through their hands before the drovers lift them and take them along the stock routes that lead to the killing pens in cities.

It is impossible to generalise on these things, but I believe the typical ringer is a type apart. A lifetime in the saddle gives him a distinctive walk. He is narrow in the hips, broad in the shoulders. He walks with a mincing step and a loose swing of the arms. Those muscles developed in walking are undeveloped in his physique, and the spread of a horse's ribs shapes the bones of his legs to a curve that is rarely found in those of a pedestrian.

They say the pubs of the Gulf Country towns would cease to exist if it were not for the ringers' cheques. Maybe so. When the ringer goes on a bender it is a memorable one.

Yet behind their toughness they are sentimentalists. I have seen them lying cross-legged on a bunk absorbed in the love stories of a woman's magazine while the dust from around the bronco panel, stirred by lassoed steers, still hangs in the air.

I saw a ringer, temporarily acting as cook, bend down and pat the head of a piccaninny who had wandered into the kitchen. The ringer was attending to a roast which he had taken from the oven.

'Look out for the fat, Billy,' he said, but his advice was lost on Billy, who solemnly watched him with a finger in his mouth.

The ringer left the stove and, lifting the piccaninny in his arms, carried him to a mattress lying in the corner, where he laid him so that he might sleep.

'Have a sleep, Billy,' he said.

But the little black boy had other ideas. Though he was obviously very sleepy he had a desire to remain erect, on the assumption, maybe, that when you are asleep you might miss something.

He rose and wandered round the kitchen again. The ringer picked him up in his arms and, without pausing in the tale he was telling me — it dealt in lurid language with a perish — he strode up and down till the little chap fell asleep in his arms. He then laid him on the mattress and returned to the roast.

Any record of the men who work the cattle stations of the north would be incomplete if it did not mention the Aboriginal stockman. It is no exaggeration to say that many cattle stations in the far north would be unable to carry on were it not for these men.

Though the Aboriginal never saw a horse until the white man came, like the Red Indian of America, he took to riding as if born to the saddle.

'Watch this man ride,' a station-owner said to me as a scrubber crashed through the gidyea, high-tailing it for freedom. We were sitting in a truck at the camp. The black that spurred in pursuit was astride a blood chestnut.

'One of the best scrub horses I've ever seen,' said the boss, referring to the horse. 'She'll stay with a beast in scrub as thick as the hairs on a dog. But watch the man on her.'

The stockman yippeed as the horse flattened into her top. She took fallen limbs and eroded water channels almost in her stride. The man on her back, his white teeth flashing in a grin of enjoyment as he drew level with the beast, sat in the saddle as if he were joined to it. He moved with the horse, helping her, it seemed, in every stride.

'Watch him lift her,' said the boss, who was enjoying it.

Horse and rider and steer went over a log together. The horse didn't lift that black; he rose with her.

The steer was labouring. In an open space the stockman began shouldering it round. It propped and skid to a stop. But no quicker than the horse that now barred its way. It turned and lumbered back to the mob.

'He's a good boy, that,' said the boss. 'I don't know what I'd do without him.'

Many station-owners wouldn't know what to do without

the blacks. Aboriginal women do the housework and the cooking, and, where they are fairly treated they do it well.

On Alexandria Station I saw Aborigines working as mechanics and pumpers. One of the engineers told me his boy could take an engine to pieces and put it together again as well as any white mechanic.

The men who work the cattle in lonely places have to have initiative, and they must be dependable. You will find these qualities in white and black.

'We like a breed with plenty of character,' a manager once told me, referring to his idea of a good herd bull.

The men who breed the cattle and who tend them during their short life have got just that.

THE DIVER

THEY boarded the plane at Rangoon, eight of them. They were big men with pale faces and they settled into their seats with relief, shrugging from their consciousness unpleasant memories and experiences they now imagined they could forget. Most of them were drunk.

The one who sat beside me sagged as the seat took his weight, then, suddenly remembering this was an ending to a personal agony, sat upright and looked out at the wide mouth of the Irrawaddy River where the wrecks of tramp steamers sunk by the Japanese on their last raid projected above the surface or lay hidden in the muddy water of the monsoon rains that discoloured the sea away out beyond the breakers.

I was working for Cathay Pacific Airways as a public relations man. The War* had just finished and I was collecting a series of impressions of some of the routes over which they would soon be carrying passengers.

The eight men were divers from New Zealand who had been taken off a salvage job on the *Niagara*, a liner sunk by a mine off the coast of that country. This job completed, the team was brought to Rangoon to clear the estuary of its wrecks and remove the danger of disease that could result from leaving decaying corpses trapped in wreckage. Now, their task done, they were returning home.

The Cathay Pacific DC3 was captained by Vic Leslie, whose conversation with the divers before we took off had

* World War Two.

revealed their occupation to me. Captain Leslie introduced me to the captain of the diving team whose concern at the moment was with his men. He greeted me, then returned to his problem. A number had refused to come on this assignment and three of those who accepted because of the big money they could earn were being left in the hospital at Rangoon where they were suffering from exhaustion and strain.

I soon found that they were not talkative men. The man sitting beside me, having looked at the wrecks flashing past our window, occupied himself with his own thoughts. He was taciturn and withdrawn but, noticing that I was looking at him with some concern, suddenly felt he should explain his attitude. He held my eyes for a moment then said, 'I've been through a bad time,' then feeling he was isolating himself from his mates by the statement, he added, 'we all have.'

'Yes,' I said.

'I don't like the thought of leaving three mates here, but they just couldn't take any more. You need to be tough. You are not meant to become companions of the dead.

'You see,' he went on, 'we had to enter some of the ships through the holes torn by torpedoes in their sides. It's not easy to do this. We had to cope with the tides . . . there were other things . . . movement is not easy in a diving costume. It was dark in those ships. We had powerful torches of course, but the beams could penetrate only a certain distance.

'We always work in pairs wherever we can. It's good to know you have a mate down there with you. But I've had them stop, then turn and make for the opening. They just looked at it. They had to know it was there. But this slowed them up. I climbed through one hole in the side of the ship where a jagged edge projected a triangle of iron out into the passageway. I had to move round it . . .

'And then there were the bodies . . .

'All the authorities wanted was to get rid of them. The War was over and no time was wasted in trying to identify anybody or give them a decent burial. The disposal of the bodies was to be left to the sea. Although this was not spelt out to us, we knew the Burmese authorities wanted a clean harbour where ships' passengers would never be horrified by the sight of a floating corpse.

'The sea was moving swiftly past the entrance to the gaping hole through which I was going to enter one of the ships. I got through this hole and my mate fed me the lifeline which I pulled behind me down a narrow passageway. With it I carried the hose which I kept coiling at different stages inside the ship. I was anxious to keep the line and the hose free of snags. The bloke I was with was new to the game and was feeling crook that morning. He had had enough.

'A lot of refugees had boarded these ships. There were women and children and old men. Some of the cabins off the passageway were full of people. They had crowded together into the room, fleeing from the sound of explosions, I suppose, and ended being jammed in cabins where they were still standing erect when the sea engulfed them.

'They had drowned in this position and their bodies had floated upwards where they hung motionless, their heads bowed under the pressure of the ceiling.

'Their drowned hair, in the light of my torch, moved like grass in a slow breeze. Their fleshless faces nodded in the light and their skeleton arms extended in a blind searching reached out to embrace companions clad in sodden, rotting clothing.

'When I thrust my hand forward with too swift a movement to push them apart, it penetrated the putridity confined behind decaying cloth and entered into softness that entrapped my gloved hand in cold decay. I experienced a moment of indescribable horror before I snatched it back from the cling of the dead and shook it clean in the water.'

He was looking down at his hand as he spoke. He must have suddenly felt ill. His face was grey. He pulled a flask from his pocket and took a swig of brandy before returning it. He wiped his mouth with the back of his hand, then shuddered in a momentary spasm and went on: 'It was my job to remove these bodies. I pulled three out into the passageway and left them standing upright there for a moment, held in position by an agitation around them, an agitation that seemed to envelop them all. I was in amongst them and felt the movement, a concerted pressure of confined water towards the door.

'I walked down the passageway, pushing water ahead of me, dividing it so that it encircled me inspired by some blind purpose that held me in a soft embrace. They responded to me taking the lead, bowing in a momentary dignity. I turned and the three that I had detached from the group revolved and began to follow me.

'The water I had liberated and set into motion moved the three bodies through the darkness behind me with what one could believe was conscious deliberation. I became giddy with nausea. I paused and placed my hand on the rust-caked wall of the cabin to steady myself. I moved towards the doorway and the silent leader of the three dead was drawn towards me by the suck of water. His swinging arm moved forward and nudged me in the back. There was panic in the movement, a fear of being left.

'As long as I live,' continued the diver, looking through the window at a featureless sea, 'I'll remember the urgency of that nudge.'

He was silent a moment, striving to control the emotion in his voice. He turned and looked at me with some appeal in his eyes, an appeal for understanding I think.

'I wouldn't have left him there,' he said. Then added in a shaking voice, 'Not after that . . .'

THERE'S A DARK MAN IN YOUR PALM, LADY

I DOUBT whether ever you feel completely at ease when confronting a fortune teller. If you are an average person, the tales you have heard of their skill will rouse in you some feeling of tension that challenges your common sense and casts doubts on your reasoning.

This is what the fortune teller wants. If you confronted him confident that he did not possess supernatural powers, or gifts you could not acquire yourself, your face would show it. Then he would not be able to rouse in you the emotions that create expressions on the face and give him the lead he seeks.

'Another tough one,' would flash through his mind and he would set to work to break down your guard and your confidence so that he could get a peep at the person behind your face.

All fortune tellers are frauds. They do not know what is going to happen to you in the future nor what has happened to you in the past. But they can guess, and this is where their skill lies—their guessing must be based on some evidence and it is in the observing and selecting of this evidence that skill is called for.

Evidence is to be found in the way a person first enters the tent or room, in their clothes, their manner, the first remarks they make. The fortune teller observes the type of jewellery they are wearing, the state of their hair, their expression, the texture of their hands (whether they are hands that have known suds or hands that have never been marked by manual work).

He looks for a wedding ring, or the mark made by one if it has been removed. An ink stain on the inside of the second finger is evidence that the person with it is in the habit of using a pen—a clerk, maybe. A nurse's hand will smell of antiseptics, the fingers of a typiste are different to those of a housewife, mechanics have hands grained with black, dairy farmers often have cracks in their hands.

The coat of an office worker is worn at the elbows, butchers are always stouter than grocers. (In my experience, anyway.) Barbers are careful with their hair, bald barbers are melancholy, lady hairdressers are easily recognisable.

Faces are revealing. There are sulky, bad tempered faces and faces that reflect a happy disposition. (A professional fortune teller once told me that people with happy faces generally have bad tempers.)

The face of a mother contains qualities not present in the face of a childless woman. Some fortune tellers claim that they can recognise the face of a woman with one child from that of a woman with a large family.

Eyes can look at a fortune teller with suspicion or with friendliness. There are women with sharp, observant eyes (they are rarely popular with other women) or with eyes that show their credulity. There are expressions of assent and denial, of fear and concealment.

All these things provide the clues from which a fortune teller builds his story.

It is not so hard, either. For many years, in my spare time, I told fortunes. I sat in tents and halls and rooms, any place where a fair was being held in aid of a hospital or charitable institution, reading palms for half a crown a time. People spend freely on fortune telling and the money I collected was always for a good cause.

The large, canvas poster that was placed above the tent or room in which I was seated, announced that 'Shabaka, the Great Egyptian Soothsayer' was seated within ready to 'draw aside the veil that conceals the future' by 'remarkable revelations.'

'All questions answered, ladies and gentlemen. For one day only. Brought here at enormous expense from his harem in Egypt, the land of mystery.'

I had barkers, too; men who agreed to spruik for nothing to increase our takings for the fund we were aiding.

I wore a Japanese kimona, a Sikh turban fastened with a Scotch thistle clasp and a scarf with a motif of Aboriginal shields—very effective.

My face and hands were blackened and I sat cross-legged on a red silk cushion with an incense burner beside me. The scented smoke that filled the tent slowly wafted out through the half-closed doorway and gave the waiting crowd the first thrill for their money.

'The Great Shabaka is now at prayer,' yelled the barker and, given the cue, I would chant in the voice of a Hollywood Egyptian, 'All-ah, All-ah, Allah, Allah,' varying the emphasis in a way I imagined would please any Mohammedans in the audience.

This preliminary being over we got down to business.

'One at a time please. No one will be missed. Half a crown for a full delineation of your character, a comprehensive outline of your past and a full revelation of your future. All questions answered. Don't push, Madam. Run away, son. Are you ready, Shabaka?'

'I am ready,' I would reply Egyptianly.

And the first victim entered, generally a woman with determination written all over her—she had to be to get in first. She was always a tough proposition. All fortune tellers agree that the first customers from a crowd are amateur dabblers in palmistry, phrenology, numerology, or any other ology, and are quick to detect variations from the traditional. They are critics of form and expect a first-class future, well delivered.

These people are particularly annoying when you are telling their fortunes with cards. They know the meanings custom gives to each card and are apt to argue with you on questions of interpretation.

I was once spreading out the cards before such a woman, a grim-faced housewife of about forty wearing a pendant representing a stag at bay. The animal had red stones for eyes and seed pearls for the rest of it. The sight of this creature glaring at me from her bosom put me out of my stride and I forgot to palm the ace of spades, the death card, which came out in a position denoting immediate death for her.

She went pale and stood up. I stood up, too. I then shook hands with her in an undertakerish sort of way and looked pensively at the floor. There was little else I could do. She knew as much as I did.

'Oh,' she said with her hand on the stag, a perfect example of understatement.

I resumed my cushion, made an exclamation, then exclaimed that I'd made a grave mistake in the shuffle in that I'd left out the Jack of diamonds which I picked up from the floor beside me.

She sat down again with a relieved expression and I reshuffled the cards. This time the ace of spades didn't come out—I was sitting on it.

But it was a close shave for her.

As far as I am concerned, the method of telling a fortune doesn't matter. I can read a foot as well as a hand and occasionally vary my usual palm reading with a spot of phrenology just for the hell of it. I can tell a fortune with both eyes shut and one hand tied behind me providing I get a good look at my victim before I close my eyes.

But, taking it all round, palmistry is the best. You can get a lot of clues from the hand and learn things never included in text books on the palm.

It always pays to tell about every third person that their hand is unique. It softens them up and they tell you more about themselves. You then repeat it back to them in different words.

Sometimes you get leads without a word being spoken.

I was telling fortunes in a marquee on Albert Park Reserve in aid of the Prince Henry Hospital some years ago, when a girl came in wearing shorts and carrying a tennis racquet.

I was just in the middle of telling her she was fond of tennis when some youngsters undid the guy ropes and the marquee fell over. It only weighed about half a ton, poles and all, they say, but it felt a darn sight heavier than that.

The girl took it very badly. She made sounds that suggested

smothering, although there was plenty of air where I was lying with my face pressed against the catgut in her tennis racquet.

After a few convulsive heaves she disappeared, crawling along a green, canvas tunnel of her own making. I lay there brooding till someone pulled me out by the leg then I went home. I'd had it. My face had a criss-cross design on it for days.

The questions put to you by clients rarely stump you though I've had a bad few seconds thinking up answers to some of them.

During the depression I was telling fortunes in the Brunswick Town Hall in aid of the unemployed when a blonde woman with a fresh complexion entered. She had not long arrived from England with a friend, she said. The friend was a French woman who couldn't speak English but who could speak Arabic. The two of them wanted to come in together but the barker stopped them. Could I speak to her friend in Arabic if she came in later?

I thought very rapidly indeed, then explained that I spoke an ancient dialect, now defunct or extinct or whatever you call it, and I was afraid my words would be unintelligible to her friend, who I presumed, spoke the Arabic of today.

She observed, rather puzzled, that this was so, and asked whether she could act as interpreter for her friend while I spoke in English. I consented to this and the friend was brought in.

She was dark and volatile and took control out of my hands. It appeared that she was travelling the world searching for her brother who, some years before, had taken a job on a boat that, after calling at a Chinese port, visited Australia before returning to France. However, the brother never returned with the boat and the question was, where was he?

I took a deep breath and tried to think where he was. I closed my eyes and drew troubled fingers across my brow and thought about how late it was and how I'd miss the last tram home if I couldn't think where he was.

I muttered, 'Allah, Allah,' twice. But it was no use. I'm blowed if I knew where he was, neither did Allah.

'Have you tried China?' I asked in a moment of illumination.

'No,' she said.

'Try it,' I said.

But it was a near thing; I just caught the tram.

The professional fortune teller, who, against the law, earns a living by reading hands, teacups or cards, gradually learns what one of them termed, in telling me about it, 'the law of average incidents'.

For instance, practically all women fall in love, have quarrels, reconciliations, lose relatives, spend unwisely and meet dark men who attract them.

Nearly every girl has had a disagreement with a boy, has loved and lost, knows a boy of whom she should beware and longs to travel. Tell them any of these things and you will be right by 'the law of average incidents'.

There is a term used by fortune tellers, 'strong-pointing', that means making a statement which may or may not be true, then following it up or contradicting it, according to the expression it brings to the face of the client.

For instance, a simple example: If you want to know whether a girl is going with a fair or dark boy you say, while looking steadily at her, 'You are going with a dark . . .' If, at this stage, her expression registers a denial, you switch quickly: 'No—a fair boy. It is a friend of yours who is going with a dark boy.'

If she now looks pleased you work from the fair boy angle, still following her expressions for guidance.

Strong-pointing can lead you into trouble but, when it comes off, you can be sure that your client will tell all her friends that you are 'Marvellous'.

After leaving a fortune teller people only remember those things they know are true.

A skilled fortune teller can always reverse a statement to his advantage if he realises he has blundered.

Once, in St Arnaud, a fortune teller had a tent at the local show. He was doing his own barking. This meant he had to finish a spiel, show clients in to the front section of his tent, dash behind the tent and enter the rear section, pull on his robe, then call out, 'Come in' to the first of his waiting customers.

It was hard work so I went up to him and offered to give him a spell by telling fortunes for half an hour while he did the barking. He was grateful and, that night, told me quite a lot about the tricks of his trade.

He always had a small hole in the side of his tent through which he could peer to see what type of companion was accompanying the person entering the tent—one always waits outside.

One day, looking through this hole, he saw a woman of about forty accompanied by a boy of about sixteen.

He was tired and when the woman came in, he failed to notice whether she wore a wedding ring or not. He started off by strong-pointing her.

'You have a son sixteen years old, Madam.'

'Pardon me, I'm single,' said the woman stiffly.

'That's so, Madam,' said the old fellow, 'this is the son you would have had if you'd married the man you were going with twenty years ago.'

He regarded this rejoinder as a good example of an escape from a strong-point proved to be wrong.

He told me I took far too long over the fortunes.

'Cut 'em down,' he kept calling into the tent.

It is hard to tell a fortune rapidly but he was a master at it.

Here are some of his observations:

'Always tell a sulky looking girl she is going to have a row with her boy.

'Tell country girls they will eventually be working in the city.

'Tell prosperous married women that their husbands will make profitable deals and they will both take sea trips.

'Tell young men they are attractive to girls.

'Tell an aged woman she has a wonderful son.

'Tell all discontented looking women that they will shortly have rows with their husbands.'

He had scores of such rules.

Standing near his tent one day, I heard a woman who had

just had her fortune told, say to her companion, 'He's uncanny, really, he is. He told me about a quarrel I had with George last week. Now, how did he know that?'

I caught a glimpse of her petulant face as she walked by and I knew how.

ALAN MARSHALL DISCUSSES
HIS WOODEN FRIENDS

WALKING on crutches was practised by the Ancients. However, in those days it was confined mainly to beggars. Nowadays, some of the most intelligent people on this earth walk on crutches. I walk on crutches.

Crutch walking may be defined as the art of leaping between two forked sticks in an effort to get somewhere.

As in every sport there are Novices, Amateurs and Professionals.

Novices are those people who are temporarily confined to crutches while nursing a broken leg or sprained ankle. Their tentative, poking method of progress brings roars of laughter from us old hands.

The Amateur is he who spends about six or seven months nursing an injury on crutches. He always poses as an authority.

The Professional is the 'lifer'—the man who will always walk on crutches. He swings along with dash and confidence and his crutches have the quality of a Stradivarius.

Crutches must be chosen with just as much care as a golfer exercises in selecting a set of clubs. Balance must be taken into consideration, the type of wood, weight.

The spring-head crutch is better in theory than practice. The top piece rests on concealed springs in tubular uprights. They are inclined to make you seasick and are only used by the inexperienced.

I favour a light, hickory racing-set with one-inch tips. They have the advantage of being both flexible and strong.

I once carelessly thrust the ends of my crutches, preparatory to leaping, in the crack between two thick planks.

I had just concluded the leap when I was flicked back again and left sitting behind the crutches which were still standing, vibrating like tuning forks.

Rocking crutches had a short life. They branched out to a rubber-studded rocker like the curved support of the old-time rocking chair. When leaping on these monstrosities one sped through the air, not only the length of a standard leap but the additional three feet or so represented by the length of the curved base. One passed people in mid-air as it were. They were only good for the city streets.

French crutches have half circles of padded steel that grip the elbow and do not extend to the armpit. They are a strain to walk on and are useless when it comes to carrying parcels.

As a means of defence crutches are excellent. The old-time Crutchy Push of North Melbourne won many a brawl with the aid of their supports. A man who was a member of this Push once gave me this advice:

'If anyone comes at you don't hit him with the crutches. You will only get one hit and then he's in on you. Poke at him—in the stomach, if you can. But best of all, bore a hole in the rest that goes beneath the armpit and fill it with lead. Keep the leaded part to the front then when arguing with a man fetch it up sharply in an uppercut to his chin. This will finish the argument.'

Only the Professionals can raise their hats while walking on crutches. The hat has to be grabbed while one is swinging in mid-air, because it is only then that one can release the grip. It is a matter of perfect timing.

You watch the friend approach. You gauge the distance between you. Right. You snatch at your hat. Dash! She has passed and is a yard behind you.

Or maybe you haven't yet reached her. Or maybe you can't grab the grip quickly enough after you have raised your hat. That's too bad. You will fall over.

I don't think a reputation for gallantry is worth it.

August was a bad month for crutch walkers. Wet pavements are slippery. All that paved portion of Swanston Street in front of St Paul's Cathedral is a trap for the unwary. After a light shower of rain no crutch tip will grip it for an instant.

I once fell over there four times in as many yards. Each time I was helped to my feet I thanked the people then waited till they dispersed, looking back over their shoulders. I then tried another leap. Down again. I got sick of it. So did the people.

There is a stone in Queen Street—just one of all the paving stones there—that seems to exude an oil. It brings you down wet or dry.

That is one of the delights of walking on crutches. You never know where you are going to fall over next.

Stairs, steps, ramps are nothing to the expert on crutches, but I have still to see the one who can manage an escalator. I have tried twice. The first time, I leaped onto the moving staircase feet first and arrived at the top without my crutches.

The next time I tried crutches first and they arrived at the top without me.

Here are a few don'ts for the beginner.

Don't poke the fire with your crutches. I do it myself, but it is a bad habit.

Don't give your crutches to the waiter to put away for you while you dine. What if someone yells out 'fire'? No. Always hang on to them.

Don't lend your crutches to a friend. If he forgets to return them you will have to stay in bed.

Don't refuse a seat offered you. Standing means leaning on your crutches with a consequent stopping of the blood circulating through your arm. You wonder why your arms go to sleep.

Don't kiss anybody goodbye at railway stations. When people get as close to you as that they are apt to kick your crutches from under you and you will end up by kissing their feet.

Don't let strangers carve their initials on your crutches. Professionals don't like it.

We are very fond of our wooden friends.

ANY MESSAGES FOR THE A.I.F.?

I BEGAN the trip with a joyful 'Gid-up'. Two seconds later I exclaimed, 'That swing-bar must have been cracked!'

Anyway, there it lay resting against Morgan's fetlocks, splintered and useless.

It was an omen, but I didn't believe in omens—not then.

I had arranged with Captain Cliff Cheong, the editor of the *A.I.F. News*, published in Cairo, to take a trip to Queensland collecting messages along the way from relatives and friends of boys in the Middle East. These were to be published in the *A.I.F. News* in a column, 'Messages from Home'. I was to rule out the 'Give my love to Johnny' type of message and concentrate on a more humorous 'Hullo'.

'They tell me your dad is wearing the pants of your blue serge suit now, Harry Digger. Well! Well!'

This was what I was after, but I had a hard job to switch mothers from the 'sending love' idea.

Pulling a caravan by car was out of the question. Petrol was not available for that. So I bought a T Model Ford, had a wagon body built on to the chassis and hitched a car caravan on behind this.

This gave me an over-all length, including the horses, of about thirty-two feet. The weight was close on two tons.

Our appearance was such that the small boys of the towns we passed through ran along beside us shouting requests for free tickets.

But I am ahead of myself. We had the swing-bar repaired and made a fresh start. Our first stop was to be Diamond Creek. It was early in January, and a wonderful day.

Well, this is what I had dreamt about. Here was the beginning of halcyon days of sunshine. Hey, ho! and the Roads of Spring! Long, tree-lined roads, lagoons with the horses grazing knee-deep in clover, the tinkle of hobble chains on moonlit nights, the leisured travel through bushland golden with wattle. The summer days of . . .

Then the brakes failed. We arrived at the bottom of that hill at a gallop.

Three weeks in Diamond Creek having new ones made, then away again.

Hey, ho! and the Roads of Spring!

'Our bad luck is behind us,' said my wife.

This remark became a cliché before we ruled it out as being in bad taste.

At Mernda, the second swing-bar broke. We repaired it with wire and on again. The roads were bare of grass; the dams were empty of water.

Towards each evening, as we drove along, we would chant: 'Trees, water, wood and grass.' This summarised the camping spot we were looking for and which we so rarely found.

The butter melted, the dust got into our honey, but we were getting messages. We hailed drovers on the road, men working in paddocks, women behind the counters of country stores: 'Would you like to send a message to a soldier in the Middle East?'

They all knew someone over there.

Away went my first despatch. The messages began to appear in the *A.I.F. News.*

At Seymour I rose early and looked out of the caravan door. Our noble steeds, where were they? I had not then learned that Jim, the elder horse, could walk just as well in hobbles as out of them. Now I know.

Three days later the police got word that they were seen eight miles out. It was night, but they drove us out to the spot in a car. There they were standing beneath a tree.

When we were putting the bridle on Jim he flinched. We struck matches and looked at him. He was covered in mud. One of his eyes was puffed and closed. His jaw was swollen like a boy with the toothache.

A man approached out of the darkness and told us that Jim had got his back fetlock caught over the hobble chain when sliding down a dry creek bed. He turned a somersault, thus the injuries. The man had released him from his trussed position.

My wife climbed on Jim's back and I slung my crutches on my arm and mounted Morgan. An eight mile ride, bareback, was in front of us. Jim was fat but Morgan was thin. I viewed the future with despair.

My wife, from Jim's broad back, talked about the moon, which was rising: 'Some day we will look back on this night as one of the most beautiful we have ever experienced,' she said.

I had placed my hands palm down on Morgan's back and was manoeuvring to sit on them. He swerved in his walk and I fell off.

'The moon,' I said caustically from the ground, 'doesn't interest me.'

We arrived back at the caravan at 2 a.m. We spent most of the next day cleaning Jim and bathing his injured eye.

Next day we made across country towards Heathcote. On the way we met an old friend who with his two companions clambered into our caravan to have tea with us. After dark a man stepped into the light before our door. He was covered in dry blood and was carrying a gun. I thought up suitable 'last words' and closed my eyes.

However, it appeared that an Italian had hit him across the face with a paling and he was just waiting for him to pass so that he could shoot him. The police arrested him later.

We landed in Bendigo with tuppence*, and had to hang round the Post Office till some cheques arrived.

With another batch of messages in my notebook we left for Echuca on a hot and sultry day. A storm was brewing. The first place where water was available for the horses was at Elmore.

We arrived there at dusk just as the storm broke. We whipped out the horses, flung on their nosebags and tied them to the fence. It was the father of all storms.

* Twopence = two pennies.

Thunder seemed to split the air just above the caravan roof. The torrential rain soon filled the slight depression in which the caravan stood.

The horses reared and reefed at their halters. I stood in the pouring rain trying to quieten them, but the water was rising higher. I clambered back into the caravan wet through.

The water rose to the floor. The wind increased in fury till, in a sudden, savage change, it hurled the caravan over as if it were a matchbox. It plunged into three feet of water amid the crash of breaking windows, falling crockery and splintering woodwork.

When we gathered our wits I was sitting on the saucepan cupboard in water up to my waist and my wife was standing on the dresser.

My crutches were somewhere under that water which was surfaced with floating manuscripts, clothing, books, tomatoes and typewriter paper.

My wife clambered through the door, now the roof, and waded off for help. I felt beneath the water for my typewriter, wireless and camera. I wrung my hands and my shirts and listened to the thunder.

Later six men pulled the caravan back on its wheels. I emerged like Neptune, and we spent the night at an hotel.

Next day we made for Echuca where we spent the following three months having the caravan rebuilt into a single unit and drying out our sodden possessions.

When, at last, we were ready to leave, Morgan refused to budge. Three months' holiday had made him collar proud. A number of men gathered to help us. They were pushing and shoving in an attempt to start him when he suddenly set off at a hand gallop with the two-ton caravan, and us in it, rocking behind him and the reluctant Jim like a ship. The next day a drover suggested I exchange Morgan for his horse. We decided on a trial. His horse ran us over a five foot bank and we narrowly escaped being tipped over.

We returned to Echuca, sold Morgan and bought Millie.

Millie was an old mare with front teeth like a row of tombstones and as narrow-minded a horse as I have ever met. But she was reliable, and we got to love her.

Two days out from Echuca she fell head over heels into an irrigation channel. She was not used to hobbles. My wife and I put a halter around her neck and hauled her out shivering with the cold.

Near Lake Boga an ominous knocking from the rear made us descend hurriedly. The back wheels were coming off. The ball bearings had been put on back to front and were chewed to pieces.

Another stay for repairs. Hey, ho! and the Roads of Spring!

At Swan Hill our little dog was poisoned.

The day before we were to leave Beverford, our next camping place, I walked across an irrigation paddock to catch the horses. I put the halter on Jim, climbed on to his back and uttered the word which began our trip, and which now was to end it as far as horses were concerned.

'Gid-up,' I said.

Jim pigrooted. After I hit the ground I knew this was almost, if not quite, the last straw.

'Look, Fate, this is coming it a bit too hot. I don't mind getting blown over in a storm, but now you've been and gone and broke me leg.'

Luckily, it was my crippled leg so I mounted my crutches and made for home, but I got bogged in the irrigated ground and had to stand there till my wife found me an hour afterwards.

Three months in the Swan Hill Hospital followed. The bone of a paralysed leg sometimes refuses to knit. It was decided to amputate the leg; then I was reprieved, my leg encased in a plaster splint, and a month ago I was discharged to allow time to try a cure.

Now I am pulling the caravan by car, but not to Queensland. I am writing this on the banks of Lake Hattah in the Mallee. The messages are now going over again, and will continue to do so until I reach Melbourne at Christmas time.

Hey, ho! and the Roads of Spring! It was worth it all.

THE THREE WISE MEN

'I'M weak,' said Jack. 'I'm weak as a dog. Nobody could be weaker than me and carry a tommy gun.'

'You had a feed yesterday,' said Fred.

'Yesterday's a long way off,' said Jack.

'And tomorrow they're dishing out turkey and ham for Christmas dinner,' said Bill.

'That's right,' said Jack. 'It's Christmas tomorrow, and here's us sitting in the middle of New Guinea in jungle as thick as the hairs on a dog. We're lost to the wide. We don't know north from south.'

'We're not in the middle,' said Bill. 'Anyway, I've got a compass.'

'What good to us is knowing where north is!' said Fred, scraping mud from his coated boots and trousers. There's nothing in the north.'

'If we reach that village I've been telling you about, we're set,' said Bill. 'It's west from here. I can tell where west is from the compass.'

'Are the Boongs there friendly?' asked Jack. 'How will they be for tucker? I tell you I'm as weak as a dog.'

'They'll have tucker,' said Bill. 'They'll have yams and taro and sago.'

'Yams are right,' said Fred. 'Yams and sago instead of turkey and ham—that suits me. Like hell, it suits me!'

'If we reach that village by morning,' said Bill, 'I'll get you to the camp for Christmas dinner. I know the way from the village. There's a ridge ahead of us, then open sandstone country, then we walk all night, then we reach the village . . .'

'Then we run into a nest of Nips,' said Jack.

'The Nips are behind the ridge,' said Bill.

'They can't be too far behind it for me,' said Fred.

'Let's get going,' said Bill. 'We've spelled long enough.'

The three men rose slowly to their feet. Their faces were drawn and wet with sweat. It ran down their foreheads and stung their eyes. The slightest exertion drenched their bodies, so that their clothes stuck to them like a clammy skin.

Around them the jungle growth was entwined in some motionless struggle. Trees bound with living ropes of green pushed their moss-covered limbs upwards, groping for the sky from beneath a canopy of tangled creepers clinging to the higher limbs of other trees.

The dank smell of decay, of rotting green, of dampness mouldering beneath fungus growths of scarlet pressed upon the three men like a weight.

They plodded through mud along a trail tunnelled through the malevolent vegetation, whose twilight mind seemed to be emerging from a vegetable state into a consciousness capable of design.

Their progress was not an unopposed movement forward, but a fight against an enemy.

They waded a creek, then plodded upwards between giant rocks behind which the country gradually cleared, and they could see the sky, now dark with night.

They rested a little, sitting in a drooping posture on stones, their heads bowed as if they were weights.

'Come on, Wise Man,' said Fred, lifting his head and looking at Bill. 'Where do we go now?'

'The village must be just about under that star there.' Bill pointed to a star shining low in the west. 'It won't be so hard now, it's open country. We'll follow that star. I know where I am now. We did a patrol through here once.'

'I got cramps,' said Jack.

'You want salt,' said Bill. 'That's what you want.'

'What I want's a feed,' said Jack. 'I want a Christmas dinner; it don't matter about the salt.'

'I'm sweating all the salt out of me,' said Fred. 'Let's get going while I got some left. That star looks good to me. A feed of yams is better than nothing.'

They rose and walked in the direction of the star, still following a track that wound between outcrops of rock and through stretches of kunai grass.

The night was empty of sound save for the ring of their hobnails on jutting pieces of stone. The three men walked one behind the other, Bill leading the way.

'Keep your eye on that star,' Jack called to him when the track made a detour to avoid a boulder.

'I'm following it,' said Bill. 'I know where we are.'

The night slid past them through hours of tramping, and it was dawn when they reached the thatched huts of the village.

The huts stood on low piles and were palisaded behind fences built to protect cultivated plots of land. No one moved in the open spaces before the huts. The village was asleep.

'Stir one of them up, Bill,' said Fred. 'You can speak Pidgin better than us.'

Bill approached a hut and climbed the steps. A native appeared at the door. He wore a white loin cloth. A sliver of bone pierced his nostrils. He looked at Bill with fear on his face.

'Three-fella longa Australia,' said Bill. 'We walk longa bush.'

'Ask him for a feed,' said Jack.

'He's scared,' said Fred. 'He thinks we're Nips. Point to where the camp is.'

He addressed the native loudly as if the man were deaf. 'We all-same good fella. Breakem head belong Jap. We belonga east. Over there, you mug,' he ended in exasperation, pointing towards the east.

'Ask him for a feed,' said Jack.

The native smiled, reassured, and spoke to Bill, who turned to the other two in explanation:

'His Mary has a baby—"Piccaninny belong Mary," he reckons. It came last night. This bird's been walking the floor.'

'Tell him I'm the doctor,' said Fred.

'Ask him for a feed,' said Jack.

'Kaikai,' Bill spoke to the native.

'Kaikai,' repeated Jack and pointed to his mouth.

They followed the man into the hut. A native woman nursing a baby sat on a grass mat beside the wall. She looked at the three men timidly, holding the baby close to her breast. The baby was the colour of honey. It moved its legs and arms.

The men sat on the grass mats that covered the floor. The native gave them sweet potatoes that had been baked on coals and they ate and watched the baby.

'Babies are not in my line,' said Jack, 'but I reckon that's a good one.'

The morning sunlight came through the doorway and rested on the baby and on the mother. The baby's head was covered with a fuzz of black hair and the sunlight was tangled in the hair so that it shone like a crown.

'That's one of the best babies I've ever seen,' said Jack again. 'P'raps it's because I was starving and I'm eating while I look at it.'

'All babies are good,' said Bill.

'What do you know about it?' said Fred.

'Not much,' said Bill. 'It's instinct.'

'Wise man, eh!' said Jack.

'We're three wise men,' said Bill, 'or we'd never got out of that jungle.'

'Don't talk jungle to me,' said Jack. 'I don't want to think about it. I was weak as a dog from sweating.'

They finished their meal and rose to go.

'We better give him something for this feed,' said Bill. 'What'll we give him?'

'Let's all leave a present for the baby,' said Jack.

They searched their pockets. They walked over to the mother and her child and bent and placed their gifts on the floor beside them.

'These are for the baby, Missus,' said Jack. 'Piccaninny belong you takem present belong us,' he added.

Upon the floor lay a pocket knife, a two shilling piece and a tin of tobacco.

The three men walked to the door and the morning sun shone full upon them.

'Christmas Day,' said Bill, taking a deep breath. 'It's Christmas Day.'

'It doesn't seem like Christmas to me,' said Jack. 'There's nothing here to remind you of Christmas.'

HALLUCINATION BEFORE DEPARTURE

I EXPERIENCED a great freedom as I ran along the flank of the hill. With every stride my arms reached for distance, pulling it towards me in festoons of green shadow. My head rose and fell with each stride.

He joined me as I reached the crest, moving in just behind me, his strides matching mine. We ran together as one. He looked at me and smiled. It was a smile that Pan would have given. It was a gateway to childhood; to what childhood was. It was clean and fragrant like the sea.

We were the same age . . . about nine I would say. He was lithe like a reed and as he leant forward to an increase of speed he curved like a bow. His arms moved like crankshafts on the driving wheels of locomotives, moving with precision and delicacy. And I matched stride for stride, breasting the flowing distance that broke upon us in waves advancing to impede us.

How beautifully we ran! How precisely we socketed upon our hips as if we were both sitting in some carriage of faery bewitched by motion. We were poised with no strain of muscle to hold us erect or brace of sinew to anchor us. We had no conflict with our bodies; we moved to the bidding of our dream.

Behind me in the shadows from which I had emerged was the hospital bed upon which I had been lying a few minutes before. This slender boy had brought a key to the unimpeded movement I was now enjoying. It clicked a release in me and the next moment I was running.

I was hallucinating, so the doctor told me when explaining my sudden escape into a world that could only have existed for me in dreams.

'You have been crippled with polio since you were six,' he said. 'You must have a great spirit to have survived till you were seventy-eight.'

He studied the thermometer he had taken from my mouth.

'You see,' he continued, 'that is why you imagined you were running. You must have always longed to run. In these feverish fantasies you have had the opportunity to realise it.'

This is how he explained it, this is how he explained that I, who had never run before, experienced how it was to run, but he didn't explain why, at the same time I got as much enjoyment from watching myself running. I was an onlooker as well as a participant; my heart had eyes and I was drenched with a surplus of beauty. Sight and movement had shared their discovery, creating a new sense of awareness in me.

I always saw running as an effortless movement in which fatigue played no part. There was no shortage of breath, no stitch, no cramping of muscle, no exhaustion. It was effortless like the gliding of a bird and brought with it a sensation of flight.

I had been hallucinating a lot lately, the effect of the many drugs I was taking. I was also weakened by high temperatures that came with the nightly sweats that drained my strength to a point where I would soon be unable to cling to the wet, streaming rock in the crevices of which my fingers clutched a fragile grip. I knew that once I was torn loose I would go hurtling down into depths that were now hidden in mist, an airless place where I would gasp convulsively for the air I needed.

There was little I could do to prevent myself slipping to the cliff's edge and falling over and over into the concealing mist; I could just lie motionless repeating over and over in my mind, 'Hang on! Hang on!' while minutes passed . . . hours . . . days . . . a lifetime . . .

But when my will failed me and I released my grip, I did not always slip to terrifying annihilation. Sometimes I would shoot away from the cliff's edge and go soaring like an eagle.

These were wonderful moments since each experience introduced me to a state I had never known before.

In these periods of revelation and enchantment I glided, I flew, I came down a steep ski run whooping with joy. The fact that all these experiences were new, experiences of which I had no memories whatsoever, did not take from them the conviction they were real. They were dream experiences born of desire and a hunger to enjoy that which, in a short time, would be lost to me for ever.

The euphoria of running had never been mine and it seemed incredible to me that I should now be running side by side with a boy who exemplified the beauty of running divorced from all effort. It was running in the abstract and there were moments when I saw it as a painting, as curved lines of merging and converging white, vibrant yet still retaining a feeling of embracement. It was love I felt as I looked at this picture of my experience, love of sight and sound and fragrance—love of life itself, of Man.

DELIRIUM

THE nurse is a white hole in the darkness. She is the smell of antiseptics and ether and her hands are wings that hover over pain.

He tossed suddenly, then lay very still as if listening. The nurse at the next bed worked in silence. She flicked the sheet above its occupant, a thin man in striped pyjamas. The sheet floated in billows above him then settled with a faint sigh. She tucked in the edges. The lantern on the floor projected the shadows of her legs across the ward. The shadows charged each other and fled . . . charged each other and fled . . .

The man who listened suddenly sat upright. His face shone with sweat. His mouth made soundless noises. His eye cried out to the nurse.

The nurse is a white hole in the darkness. She is the smell of antiseptics and ether and her hands are wings that hover over pain.

The nurse with a blanket held in her hands stood motionlessly watching him. She lay the blanket on the end of the bed. She walked round to him clothed in shadow and lamplight.

'Lie down,' she said, gently. She placed her hand upon his wet forehead. He muttered and lay down. Her hand followed his head to the pillow and rested there. He drew great shuddering breaths of air.

'I will make your pillows higher,' she said.

'I am suffocating,' he gasped.

'I will make your pillows higher.'

She placed an arm behind his back and raised him. He laughed weakly then suddenly began talking to himself. She stacked pillows behind him. He sank back upon them.

'Is that better?'

'The perfect plot,' he muttered. 'The perfect plot.' He suddenly grasped her wrist with his hand and looking into her eyes said tensely, 'Death loves you.'

She did not remove her untroubled gaze. She watched him, quietly smiling. 'I love you more than death.'

'Sh-sh-sh,' she whispered. 'Go to sleep now.'

He lay very quietly. She left him and returned to the next bed. The thin man had been watching them.

'He talks about that perfect plot all day.'

'He is very ill.'

'What is he?'

'He is a writer. He writes stories.'

'He must be in love with you,' the thin man smiled at her. The blanket she had flung above him faltered in the air as if the power that guided it had been suddenly withdrawn.

'He is very ill,' she said.

She smoothed his bed. She lifted the lantern from the floor. 'Will you call me if you think he needs me? I am going out to get something to eat.'

'Goodo,' said the thin man.

She left him, swinging her lantern. She raised it as she passed the writer's bed. His restless eyes glittered in its light.

'Go to sleep,' she whispered. She was gone.

My white pain-flower. My moving mist that trails a lantern. Whose lips are hands, red, fingerless and sweet, that clutch the mouths of favoured ones.

In the dark there moved through the ward a restlessness like drifting air. There was a tossing of bodies, a creaking of beds, faint moans and sighs. The walls had retreated; the corners were caverns of darkness and pain like drifting air. There was a tossing of bodies, a creaking of beds, faint moans and sighs. The walls had retreated: the corners were caverns of darkness and pain like a large bat fluttered forth and hovered over those who moaned.

'Tis death she loves. Green laughter shakes his sweatless hide as on the galloping hooves of pain he drums my bed—he drums my bed—he drums my bed. —

The writer raised himself on his elbow. The thin man was

asleep. The writer could see faces; cruel evil faces that
advanced from the darkness with dripping froth-rimmed
mouths, that snarled and muttered and champed their jaws
then faded into nothingness.

And kisses like pale frightened birds that speed the hawk flew
from death's mouth. Ah, my moving mist that trails a lantern.

He peered with sudden fear across the ward. From among
the sweating trees they came; in little groups they came,
their tragic faces gleaming like lacquered copper amid the
steam that rose from the mud through which they waded.

He knew them all—the Old Man and his dog, Madam
Judge O'Men, Dink Adams, the Factory owner, Rose Anne,
Ah Ling Foo, the Machinist, Silly Mary—There were others.
He had created them. In his stories he had created them.
From vague, intangible whirls of mist he had shaped them.
Into their empty, open mouths he had flung a tongue. They
spoke the words born of his mind—*Ah Jesus keep them from me.*

There was a large, cleared space separating him from the
slippery trees. They skirted this and kept pace with him as he
plunged desperately away from them. But he too was in mud
and though he made frantic efforts, he could move but slowly.

He paused panting. They stood in a group at the edge of the
trees. They shouted and shook their hands above their heads.
They agonised together, their faces twisted as from torture.

He moved on with painful labour. They moved with him.
He ceased struggling. They advanced upon him. Their
anguished eyes entreated. He did not understand. They shook
their fists: 'Kill us,' they cried. 'Finish our story.'

They gathered round him. Their mouths were open. Dank
hair dripped sweat. He breathed the steam of their bodies.

They bent over his prostrate, muddy form. 'Kill us. Finish
our story. There is only one perfect plot.'

They swayed their bodies and began chanting, 'It begins at
birth and ends in death—It begins at birth and ends in death—
It begins at birth and ends in death—'

He shrank from them.

'I have loved you all,' he said, faintly. 'I cannot kill you.'

'You must,' they entreated him. 'Every living creature
carries with it the perfect plot. And you have left our stories

unfinished. We are incomplete. We can never die. Finish our story. It begins at birth and ends in death,' they again chanted.

The old man stepped forward leading his dog. His face was wistful. His trousers were caked with the yellow clay of his mine.

'This 'ere dog's a good dog,' he said to the writer. 'He is a good dog and you have left us. And me with the flower, the Iris bloom that is blue in front of me hut, and you have left us. Me and the Iris flower and the dog.'

'You are my friend, old man,' cried the writer, hoarsely. 'I love you and the dog and the Iris flower that is blue in front of your hut. And I saved your nephew's life with the help of the dog; and I left you and your nephew and the dog sitting eating in the hut and you were happy.'*

'The perfect plot,' said the man vaguely, looking round at the silent, listening group; 'The perfect plot that finishes our story—'

'Kill him,' cried the others angrily. 'Finish his story.'

'No. Not that,' pleaded the writer. He sank lower in the hot mud. 'Not that.'

They talked angrily together and looked at him with hate in their eyes. Sweat rolled from their faces. They waded round him pointing and shouting.

Madam Judge O'Men harangued them. The creases that split her cheeks drained her streaming face. She sobbed and screamed her words.

'He left me in the rooms behind the shop of Ah Ling Foo in Little Lon. I takes the money and it's all respectable like. And he,' her outstretched hand accused the writer, 'sends in a mug from the bush, and the mug hops into Harry the Bludger and beats hell out of him. And he leaves us. And Harry the Bludger bein' beat up and me watchin'—Oh, God save us! And the girls that have helped me—And always that way it will be—me watchin' and the girls that have helped me.'†

She turned in a fury on the writer. 'Finish the story, blast you,' she screamed. 'You and your perfect plot.

* 'The Dog', *The Complete Stories of Alan Marshall*, Nelson, page 97.
† 'The Teeth of Ah Ling Foo', *Flame Magazine*, November 1936.

Finish it. Finish it.' She fell back panting.

Dink Adams with bearded face clutched his lank throat with a thin, dark hand. 'It is the breath of me that is going,' he gasped to the machinist beside him. 'He gave us breath,' she said. 'Once, he gave us breath.'

'I am a murderer,' he said. He nodded towards the writer sinking slowly deeper into the mud. 'He left me with Annie and she was still. And it was the police that were knocking at the door. And me after killing the life of her. Will he finish my story?' he demanded. 'Will he finish it?'

She gestured vaguely.

He turned from her hopelessly.

'He put himself into my story,' she said. 'He was a singer and he loved me.'

The writer struggled to speak to her. The mud sucked him deeper. Steam floated past his face. 'I am not a singer now.'

'You loved me. Finish our story,' she pleaded.

'You are a nurse now,' he said excitedly. 'A nurse with a lantern. I still love you. You will be many things. But I will always love you. It will be the perfect plot. I . . .'

But the others cried out at the words. They rocked and chanted. 'It begins at birth and ends in death. Kill her.'

They crowded upon him malevolently so that he cried out and placed an arm across his eyes.

The factory owner intervened.* He waded forward and stood before the writer panting, his hand over his heart. 'Am I to be left with the machines?' he said, hoarsely. 'The machines that beat—that beat—'

'Yes,' shouted the writer with sudden strength.

'Lead me through my office,' cried the factory owner, 'through my office to my death. I want the papers and the balance sheets that I know. I am standing with my workmen among machines that beat—that beat—'

'Help him to die,' they all cried.

'People,' said the writer, weakly, 'I made you from shadows in my mind. I put words into your mouths and watched you develop into what you are. And I loved you. Is not that enough? Other people know you now. You are mine no longer. You will live in the minds of others who will finish your story as they will.'

* *How Beautiful are thy Feet*, Penguin.

'Traitor! Deserter!' they spat at him. They spent themselves in a fury of invective. They clung to each other. They moaned and swayed on their feet, their suffering faces glittering with sweat.

The writer began to tremble. His head fell back exhausted on the mud. He closed his eyes a moment. The people gathered round him whispering. He gazed at them unmoved, too tired for effort.

Their faces changed and became full of kindliness. They bent and caressed his face with their fingers. 'See, he is writing his own story. Leave him.'

They backed away smiling and waving their hands. They dissolved into shadows and disappeared among the wet trunks of smooth trees. He was alone sinking deeper into the mud.

The nurse is a white hole in the darkness and the pat-patterings of her slippered feet scurry like mice around the sepulchral beds that clasp the dead that will not die. My moving mist that trails a lantern.

The thin man awoke. He raised himself suddenly. The writer's quilt rose and fell to laboured breathing. He sobbed beneath its canopy.

'Nurse,' called the thin man. 'Nurse.'

She hurried in holding her lantern aloft.

There was no sound of sobbing from the writer's bed. The quilt was still.

It begins at birth and ends in death . . . It begins at birth and ends in death . . . It begins . . .

THE LITTLE BLACK BOTTLE

HE RAISED himself stealthily, quietly, like a ghost. He propped himself on his elbow and stretched his incredibly thin and scraggy neck the better to view the long ward.

The night nurse was sitting before an open fire, resting. Her immense shadow danced behind her on the tall white wall. It shook and swayed as if seized with uncontrollable laughter. It leaped to the ceiling as she bent forward to poke the logs and hovered over her like a thwarted witch barred from her cauldron.

She sat there unmoved, her chin resting on her hand, her elbow on her knee.

Old Alex watched her with sharp, eager eyes, his lips moving in unspoken words. Sparse grey hair, ruffled by the pillow and fine as silk, floated round the brown dome of his head. At each movement of the nurse he thrust his head forward as would a pointer dog that sights game.

Suddenly fear squeezed his face with cold hands. He turned quickly to the shadows behind him. He whimpered aloud and shrank in his blankets. Then anger seized him. He sat up and shook his clenched fist poised on the end of his fleshless arm like a death-shamming spider. He mouthed imprecations and curses at something that watched him from the darkness of the corner. He gibbered impotently from his bed.

For William was there. He knew. He could see him at nights when sleep should have made him blind. William with his red-mouthed throat running blood and his lips awry.

It was not shadows that he saw. No, not shadows. For shadows were intangible things; but the face of his mate was warm with life. It moved, and wrinkles that he knew engraved the brown skin. The small white scar upon the neck alone was still. Once bending over him as he slept he had seen it; staring at him in its stillness.

Ah! but when the slashed skin shot back it, too, had moved; had shrunk and quivered and—Oh, God pity him! It was only sleep he needed. Sleep from the little black bottle.

The night nurse had risen from her chair. Firelight pattered on her apron with red fingers. She looked down the ward.

Old Alex sank quietly back on his pillows like a penitent dog; but his eyes gleamed angrily as he peered from beneath the blankets he had pulled over his head.

The nurse was in league with William. Why did she keep from him the sleep that rested in the little black bottle? For sleep was a glorious darkness where William did not gibber and gesture with accusing hands.

He had not meant to kill William. No! As God was his witness. Had he not had gold enough in the little canvas bag beneath his bunk that night when William died? Then why did William haunt him now with his bloody throat agape and the whites of his eyes glittering in the dark like the fangs of a snake?

It was so many years ago. Now when he was old and ill why should William return, still young, still carrying the superb, unwasted muscles of youth and whisper that he had killed him? Killed him—No! No! He would not harm his mate. It's true he had taken the razor and bent over him in the darkness. But what of that? He had not wakened William. William's breath was slow and regular—slow and regular— slow and—No, by the Saints! It whistled from his throat in shrill bubbles; it fled from him in panic. And upon the hand that held the blade—his hand—No! not his hand—not his— Nurse!—

He flung back the blankets. His sunken face shone vulture-like. Sinews on his throat twitched like the tortured strings of a violin. Upon his brow there glimmered cold beads of moisture.

The nurse's eyes were unhurried. 'Now! Now! What is the matter?' she asked.

'The little black bottle,' he gasped. 'Bring it to me. It makes me sleep. I must sleep. Just a little drop.'

The nurse placed the lantern on the floor and commenced tucking in the blankets.

'No more tonight,' she said, firmly. 'You have had one dose. Too much is bad for you. You lie back and try to sleep without it.'

'I tell you I cannot sleep without it,' he shouted.

'Be quiet. You will wake the other patients.'

'It's a little black bottle.'

'I know. I know. Lie down.'

He rocked his body from side to side and shook his clenched fists feebly.

The nurse stood for a moment looking thoughtfully down at him. She held the lantern closer to his face, looking at his eyes. She placed her hand on his head and said, 'Go to sleep, there's a good chap.'

But when she had left the ward he suddenly felt the touch of hands upon his blankets and knew that William had returned. He cowered lower into the warmth of his bed clothes and whimpered to himself.

'No, William. No. I did not kill you. I loved you, William. Do not touch me with your hands. Please. Please. They are cold; cold like death. What's that? Eh! Eh! What's that?'

He started up and stared with wide eyes into the darkness.

'Sleep, William, sleep? You will give me sleep?'

A smile was on his face. His teeth shone. Specks of light glowed from his eyes. He stretched out his emaciated hands as if in welcome. His voice was eager.

'Ah! The little black bottle. You will give it to me. I will sleep. You are good, William, good.'

He threw back the blankets.

'It's only a little black bottle. I will follow, William. It is sleep.'

The flames from the fire flung shadows on the floor. They locked his eager feet and retreated in panic. He shuffled falteringly down the ward, a thin arm outstretched, his eyes shining.

Before him the white cupboard against the wall stood upright like a tomb.

He tottered towards it, grasped its handle.

A shadow moved between him and the fire. He became lost in a moving darkness. The door of the cupboard swung open.

His voice came, quaveringly.

'Thank you, William. Only a little drink. It brings me sleep. I did not kill you, William.'

There was silence, then a scream, loud, hideous, unrestrained; a crash, a thrashing of arms upon the floor, a convulsive gasping for air—

'Prussic acid,' said the doctor, after examining the little black bottle. 'He evidently thought it contained his sleeping draught. The bottles are similar. Poor devil!'*

* This was the first story published under the name Alan W. Marshall in 1934.

STORY-TELLING

I HAVE been living in a caravan in the bush over the last few months. It is a lonely place. There are kangaroos there and possums and I have plenty of time to commune with myself. Under such circumstances you become a pupil to yourself and I feel that one could not get a better teacher than oneself. I often tell myself things that I didn't know I knew. But mainly when looking out of the window of the caravan, before putting my pen to paper, I follow a track of interest, rather than revelation, in my thoughts and it is this track I'm going to follow tonight in my talk.

I have retreated to this caravan to get away from the phone, and to write a fairy story — a book, a fairy book. Now why I am writing a fairy tale at this stage of my life I am not quite sure, but I think I know the incident that triggered it. I was travelling with my daughter in Hungary. She is eighteen years old. And we stopped sometimes at hotels in remote places where we shared the same room. While she was lying in bed reading C. P. Snow's *Corridors of Power*, I was lying in another bed reading Hungarian fairy tales, and one of us would lower the book and say 'Listen to this' and later on the other one would say the same, and it was with some irritation that we each listened to the other's quotation. But I did quote this to her which made her drop *Corridors of Power* for a moment, not in disgust at *Corridors of Power* I think, but at my fairy stories. But this was the opening to the fairy story that I read then.

'Once upon a time a long time ago, beyond the seven seas

and even further than that, there lived an old woman in a crack behind a stove. In the twenty-third fold of her dress lived a white flea. In the white flea was a city in which lived a beautiful princess.' Now that seemed to me a magnificent opening to any story.

The story had nothing to do with the flea or the old woman or the crack behind the stove, but it had everything to do with the fairy princess. So I decided that I would like to write a fairy tale when I came back about a fairy princess and about dragons and about giants, and I wanted it set in Australia—because in my experience children still like those stories.

So I would like to say something about this fairy tale because it has a bearing on many of the things that have been discussed at this conference. The story is called *The Magic Leaf** and it is the story of a little boy in the Australian bush who lives with Crooked Mick, an Australian folk hero. But he decides to set off to find a beautiful princess he can rescue from a dragon. Before he goes, the South Wind leaps out of a storm cloud and talks to him and he says to him, 'I will make you a present that will help you on your journey,' and he gives the boy a magic leaf. He says, 'This leaf will replenish itself but when you give it to people—to cruel people—they will become kind. When you give it to people of whom you are afraid, they will become kind too. It will make plain people beautiful and sad people happy. So be generous with the leaf.'

And the little boy says, 'What does the leaf mean?' and the South Wind said, 'It means—I love you: you are loved: you are needed.' So equipped with this leaf the little boy sets off on his journey accompanied by a kangaroo that has the remarkable power of being able to take anything he likes from his pouch. It is a magic pouch.

There are many adventures but they come to a land of clutching grass, and the land of clutching grass lies on a plain beyond which is a country of green hills and lovely bush. And there is a vast crowd of children waiting to cross this land of clutching grass—clutching grass and whispering

* Published as *Whispering in the Wind*, Nelson, 1969.

grass—and as the children walk through it it keeps whispering to them, 'You are too fat.—You are too thin.—Straighten yourself up.—Why are you so stupid? Why aren't you like the little boy next door? I have spent a lot of money on your education. You must do better. You must do this. You must do that. You must be this. You must be that. You must straighten yourself up.' And gradually the grass twines around their legs and pulls them down and sometimes destroys them. But when the little boy gives each child a leaf (you are loved—you are needed) they walk across the grass unharmed.

And when he eventually finds the beautiful princess, she is imprisoned in this terrible tower by a cruel king and a wicked queen because she cannot pass her Intermediate, her Leaving or her Matriculation.* So the little boy presents her with the leaf (you are loved—you are needed) and she immediately passes her Intermediate, her Leaving or her Matriculation. She is guarded by a bunyip who was trained at a dragon school, and who was expelled because he couldn't breathe fire, but he is the dragon that shoots water from his nostrils, and he is the one that helps the little boy to find the beautiful princess—and that is the story.

When I began writing this I tried various styles that I felt would suit the tale I wanted to tell, and I realised that I was foolish and I began writing in the way that is natural to me.

Now it seems to me that it is as if a writer sometimes lives in a room: it is the room of his immediate surroundings and he has to get to know that room very well. Sometimes he turns on a torch and illuminates one spot in the room, and that is a short story. Now other writers press a switch that floods the room with light and that is a novel, and others fling open the windows onto the wide world and the sun outside comes in, and then not only is the room illuminated but the world beyond it also and that is a great novel: that would be *War and Peace*.

But the illumination supplied by literature to readers has first of all to be supplied to the writer by life. Galsworthy

---

* These are no longer public examinations in Victoria where the Higher School Certificate, which replaced Matriculation, was first examined in 1970.

once said, 'Live first, and write afterwards.' These moments of illumination that form the material for future writing begin when you are a child. I remember when I was a child going out and kneeling on the grass and digging my fingers into the grass and breathing the smell of lichen and moss into my lungs. I remember chasing rabbits with a dog that scooped them up into its jaws, and holding the little limp body in my hands, and there was blood on my hands, and that was my first association with death. And then a dog I loved died and all the world seemed full of despair—and those are the moments that you never never forget.

My daughter—my little daughter—I was driving her along once and we saw a dead cat and she said to me, 'There is a perfectly good cat someone has thrown away.' Her idea of death was different. But that was a moment of illumination for her.

And then I was trying to merge myself with life, to understand what I was seeing, to become part of the whole earth in which I live, part of the people, and I went for a ride on a little white pony with my two little daughters. And the smallest one was sitting on the back with her legs so short that they were thrust out and were parallel with the ground, and she was almost in danger of being pushed over the back. And I was sitting precariously in the centre and the other one was sitting on the withers, and it was September and the wattle was out. It was springtime and we were on a journey of adventure. And I said to them, 'Something will happen today,' and I felt that surely on this wonderful day, being carried along so marvellously by the little white pony, that there would be a tremendous blaze of light or we would see kangaroos or emus or Aborigines or some fairy or something.

And we came to a clearing and we all dismounted and I said to them, 'Now listen. We will stand very still. I think it will happen here.' And we stood very still and the sun beat upon us and we could smell the wattle.

And I said, 'What do you hear? Do you see anything?' And one of them said, 'You know, behind every tree I am sure there is a little man with a blue jacket and red trousers, and when you turn away he pokes his head from behind the tree and watches you, and as soon as you turn around he pulls his head back and you never see him. But I am sure there is one behind every tree.' And that is how I felt the bush spoke to me, and that was a moment of illumination when I felt she had suddenly given to me a picture of the bush.

Another little boy I was walking with in the bush—he had a muffler on: his mother always thought he would catch his death of cold—and I said to him, 'There is a great box tree. It's a gentlemanly tree. I'm not very fond of it, it's well dressed and very smug,' and he didn't make any comment. And then I said, 'There is a stringy bark tree. It is a bit untidy but I rather like him. I know him very well. I often come down here and speak to him.' And we came to Casuarina, a she-oak, and I said to the little boy, 'This is a very sad tree,' and then he made his only remark on the day's walk and he said, 'It is not the tree that is sad, it is you.' I never went for a walk with him again.

A writer experiences more of these moments than most people because he seeks them. This is the stuff of his writing. He has to learn to describe things not from what he sees but from what he feels. I see life often as a series of peaks divided by flat plains. Now these peaks are the moments of illumination, the moments of truth, when something of great significance happens to you and you never forget them. The plains are the ordinary days when we go to and fro from school or to work and back again when nothing very exciting happens. But when you are writing your autobiography you pull all the peaks together, draw them in until they are touching. So a book that is written about any one man's life is a description of the peaks. It is condensed. And a novel too can be written in this way, when one first of all jots down all the peaks that one wishes to describe and then joins them together. But it is only one way.

I have spoken to many writers and writers often believe that there was a stage in their life when they were capable of making a decision whether to become a commercial writer, a writer of literature, or a writer in the prevailing fashion. I heard one writer say once that he intended to shock his way into recognition. And some decide to write in an obscure and complex way, believing that this method will establish them as being profound. And others avoid simplicity like the plague since it might be construed as naïvity. But I doubt whether any writer has ever been in the position to make these decisions with any hope of success.

A book built on foundations selected by a desire for acclaim or quick recognition is rarely a work of literature. I think a writer is bound to a certain style and attitude by conditioning, temperament and emotion, and I don't think he can betray these deep-seated aspects of his personality to the extent of finding fame and appeal for which he is not suited. You have to be true to your last. The writer who told me he was going to shock his way into recognition got the recognition he sought. He was talked about and praised and condemned but his book, written to shock, is never read today. Yet he was really a lyrical writer; he was sensitively attuned to the world around him and basically I think a romantic. In this field he could have written a very good book.

And those who try to be obscure for obscurity's sake, believing that the personal image is more important than the universal one, will never write books of permanent value. Writers whose obscure or complex books are an outstanding success can write in no other way. That is their natural style, and even if we cannot completely understand them we nevertheless have to respect them. I think Patrick White is a symbolist. He has a prose style that is unusual and peculiar to himself. He is a sincere and talented artist. He expresses himself in a way that comes naturally to him. You may like or dislike him, but you respect him.

I remember a friend of mine very many years ago—when surrealism was discussed and written and painted—who used to write for a French publication, and he would send these pieces over and have them published in France. And he used to try and persuade me to make my mind blank and write exactly what I was thinking, which seems to be a contradiction. However, I did sit down one day and wrote two pages while he was standing near me—just any words that came into my mind. I think one of the sentences was 'Ducks and clouds were rumbling,' or something like that, which led him to remark later that he wondered what influence ducks had on my life. But after I had finished it he said to me he thought it was very good, and he liked it, and sent it over to France where it was published. He said he used to believe in the release of the subconscious, but he was really a victim to sound and image. It was the bizarre, the odd, the strange, that appealed to him. It did not appeal to me, but he was never a fake when he wrote in that way. He was a sincere writer, but when I tried to write that way I was a fake. Writing is the man.

I read so many books today that are not an expression of the man but an expression of his ambition or of a manufactured intention. Writers are sometimes amazed at what critics read into their work. Sometimes the critics are right and sometimes they are wrong, but there are times when a writer, in seeking to establish a moment or evoke a mood or present a viewpoint, uses images and situations that may be springing from his subconscious. Then what he writes reaches out beyond the intent of his prose and reveals attitudes and uncovers motives of which he is probably unaware. The critic may see them or the critic may make a mistake and show that he does not understand what the writer is aiming at, but if the critic attributes to him something profound the writer congratulates himself on this.

I remember writing a story about duck shooting* because I hated people shooting ducks for sport and some critic had described it as an allegory of war and peace and a writer friend of mine, speaking through the side of his mouth, said, 'Don't deny that Alan.' So it was probably much better if it were claimed as an allegory. Professor Hope in that wonderful book *The Cave and the Spring* has a chapter dealing with this in his poem 'Imperial Adam', showing how three critics treated it differently.

When I was in Russia I met a very great man called Marshak† who was eighty-four—he's dead now—and he told me about the story of his childhood which he had written. He said the critics all dealt with it as a story of his childhood

* 'My Bird', *The Complete Stories of Alan Marshall*, Nelson, page 220.
† Samuil Yakovlevich Marshak, 1887–1964.

and he said, 'That was not my intention.' He said, 'What I wanted to do was to write a book to show what childhood meant.' He was a very great translator, and he told me that he visited Scotland where he studied Burns for some years and then came back and translated Burns into Russian. Over in China they had no scholar who understood Scottish words, so they translated Burns into Chinese from Marshak's translations. So Marshak told me he was waiting for an Englishman to go over and translate them back from Chinese into English again and there would be some magnificent new poems.

I sometimes feel there is always a temptation for a writer to use his work as a vehicle to snatch a victory from past lost arguments or to flay someone he dislikes or to put in the dock living characters who offend him. If he uses his work as a vehicle to get rid of personal animosity it will be detected by the critics—there's something phoney about it, it seems to be too heavily loaded.

I think that sometimes a writer is completely unaware of how he gets his effect. I've read articles on Henry Lawson that pay tribute to his great skill as a short story writer and proceed to prove from one of his stories that he approached it like a chess player, conscious of the effect of every move, conscious of every overtone and undertone, constructing it under the guidance of a mind that had made a profound study of the short story as an art form. Well, I don't believe this. I think that Lawson was a natural story writer—story-teller—and in his best stories he made few mistakes because he couldn't. The story develops in his mind as a tale told to himself and the most effective words and phrases came naturally in saying what he wanted to say. He would certainly write and re-write some of his stories and change sentences and sequences sometimes, but I think he would be guided in such cases by an instinctive sense of fitness—a knowledge of the evocative power of certain words, their fall.

Regarding that word 'fall'. My father used to plait stock whips from kangaroo hide, and when he had finished the lash he would fasten it onto the handle and throw it forward in a curve, and the lash would curve gracefully in a bow and then the end would fall on the ground. He called that the 'fall' and he would say to me, 'This whip has a wonderful fall.' And some whips had a bad fall. But when he made a whip and it fell beautifully he'd be very proud of it. Once he had read something I had written and he said to me, 'The words fall beautifully.' It was like the fall of a whip. I often think of that when I'm reading good prose and I see how the words fall.

Lawson in his stories used to remember significant incidents and then he would describe them and build on to them to give them a meaning. Chekhov remembered incidents too, but he used them as a springboard to launch himself to great heights where his view encompassed the world. And Gorky was confined like Lawson to personal experiences, yet he gave them wings. Gorky was a great note taker, and it is the taking of notes that has always interested me and I have always placed great value on it. I have recorded dialogue and character studies, not only in a book or short story, but because the recording of them enlarges my knowledge and it impresses it firmly upon my mind so that it is available even when its source is forgotten.

When I was in Russia I saw some of Gorky's notes. I visited a writer, Chukovsky,* a man of about eighty-four, who had been great friends with Gorky and who had received many letters from him, and who, with Gorky, had started children's libraries throughout the Soviet Union. He told me that Gorky was an amazing story-teller—a marvellous man to listen to—and he told me that Gorky was telling him one night of how he was on the banks of the Volga at night time. It was dark and he heard a man shouting from the centre of the river and Gorky tore off his boots and jumped into the river, and swam out to where the man was struggling and splashing, and he went to help him. And the man said, 'What's the matter with you?' and Gorky said, in effect, 'Aren't you in need of help?' 'No I am not,' he said. 'This is none of your business.' He said, 'Can't a man shout from the middle of the river without you interfering? I have always wanted to shout from the middle of the river and I am going to shout from the middle of the river.' So Gorky swam back

* Korney Chukovsky pseudonym of N. I. Korneichuk, 1892–1970.

again, but as he walked away he kept thinking of the strangeness of human beings. How odd they are.

But Chukovsky told me this story and said, 'I don't like the writings of Gorky — I think he was a much better teller of tales.' Well, this surprised me, and when I was in Hungary I said to an interpreter — I had a woman, a very clever woman — I said to her, 'When Chukovsky told me that he didn't like the works of Gorky, he suddenly fell in my estimation.' And then she said this to me, a remark I can't forget. She said, 'The fact that Chukovsky does not like the works of Gorky does not detract from Chukovsky's stature nor does it detract from Gorky's.' And then she added, 'I have known great men and cultured men who dislike Beethoven.'

She was an extraordinary woman, this woman. She told me four things that I can't forget. I had many conversations with her but it is like looking for something illuminating, and these four remarks she made I have always remembered. The first is about Chukovsky that I have just told you.

Another one was this. I went out to see Hungarian wild horses. There are about eight of them left and they tried to breed them back. And she was interpreting for me, and she was a dark woman with very high cheek bones and almond eyes, and she used to tell me that Hungary had been the cockpit of the world and armies had gone over there and passed through there, and they were a mixture of all races — Greek, Roman, all of them — and that there was no really typical Hungarian. But she had these high cheek bones and slanting eyes, and we were looking at these horses, these eight horses, and the dorsal mark down their spine was black. I was talking to the director and I told him I thought I had been told in Australia that that is a sign of endurance, and he agreed. But when I went around to their heads I said, 'Look, they have got Mongolian horses' heads.' He was indignant about this and he said, 'No, they haven't. There is no Mongolian blood in these ponies.' He said, 'Maybe millions of years ago, but they are the pure Hungarian wild horse.' But when I was walking away with this woman I said to her, 'The stallions of Genghis Khan left foals all across Europe, you know.' And touching her cheek she said, 'So did his soldiers.' This is one remark I remembered.

Another remark she made. I was sitting in front of a log fire with her and she said, 'This is medieval television.'

There was a certain type of academic in Budapest she didn't like very much, who speaks a number of languages but who talks, so she said, nearly like the pages of a book repeating the words of other men. And she said to me, 'Here comes an idiot in six languages.' They were the only remarks I can remember she made.

I have always believed that the dialogue in the book of a writer who takes notes like Gorky took them is more convincing than when the dialogue is merely created from knowledge of the character. And I have read that Dickens took notes. Now if this were not known I think it would be evident from his dialogue. Although note taking is nearly always a sign of a young writer full of enthusiasm, Somerset Maugham was one of the few writers who continued it until he was an old man.

I haven't taken many notes for some time but I was talking to a young man the other day who came into my room. I just jotted down one thing he said. He was employed by a council at one of these dance halls where a number of tough characters go, and he was telling me that at the entrance to the doorway of this hall there is a step an inch high. He said the sober men who come in there are always falling over this step flat on their faces, but, he said, when the drunks come in they never fall over this step and then he added, 'Drunks, you see, step high like a show pony.' It seemed suddenly to give a picture of these people.

Well, selection is the key to recording actual dialogue and there is rarely much gold in the dish you are panning, but I used to seek for those remarks—one remark, that flashed like a light—and then you see the man that he is, revealed. You may listen to a person for half an hour, and it may be a conversation that is not the stuff of a book, and then he makes one remark and that's it. I remember standing in the street where a girl had fainted on the steps of a bank and a crowd, a little knot of people, gathered around her, and there was one man there who kept saying, looking around at the others as if he had been there first and wanted to show that he knew all about this sort of thing, 'It is always the same. I have seen it happen.' Then he would turn away and say, 'Yes, it is always the same. I've seen it happen.'* For some reason or other he suddenly established himself. I knew him very well. It didn't mean anything, but he kept repeating this. I don't know exactly what he meant.

Another man I remember, an old miner, who used to live on a disused mining field. And I used to call in to see him when I was passing in the caravan. He lived in an old hut with an old red gum tree at the door and against the gum tree were the remains of an old iron bedstead, the ruins of a buggy, and horseshoes, and a set of harrows, and he used to sit at the door of his hut. And when I drove up I'd walk in there, and all around him were the shafts and the mullock heaps of this old mining field. And he used to say to me, 'Are there any new murders lately?' And he did not ask that because he had a morbid interest in murders, but because when he was young and the mining field was in operation two men lived in a hut not very far from his hut. And one night one of them rose and hit the other with a log of wood and killed him, and carried his body on his shoulder up the mullock heaps and threw his body down a shaft. And he was interested in murders from then on. But I said to him one night, sitting over the wide open fireplace with all the charcoal on the hearth, 'I wonder why he did it,' and he said, 'Well, I don't know. But it was winter time. You see, they had been sitting over a log fire together, and they had been living together for years. And one of them spat in the fire noisily, and when he did that the other one would give a gesture of disgust. Then half an hour would pass. The first would spit in the fire again and the other man would show his disgust. He would do that week after week, month after month, year after year, till finally he killed him.'

I thought that was something but he said to me, 'Would you like to see this shaft?' and I followed him up on the foot of these mullocks where thin stringy bark saplings were growing up, and passed through the thin wild grass until we

* 'Street Scene at Midday', *The Complete Stories of Alan Marshall*, Nelson, page 213.

came to a level patch on top of one of the mullock heaps. And I looked down the wide gaping hole of a deep shaft from whence came a cold draught of air that smelt of frogs and deep, dark stagnant water way down there. And I threw a stone down, and you could hear it bounce on the sides. Then dead silence. Then the sudden splash way down — terrifying. And standing there thinking of what happened so many years before I was reconstructing it for my own benefit and I said to him, 'What time did it happen?' He said, 'In the middle of the night.' I said, 'Was the man he killed very heavy?' He said, 'Yes, he weighed about twelve stone.' I said, 'The other man must have been strong to carry him up here.' and he said, 'Yes, he was.' I said, 'I wonder how he carried him.' He said, 'Oh! He would carry him in the fireman's lift, with one arm down over his shoulder holding that, and his legs dangling down at the back.' I said, 'It would be very hard to see in the dark.' He said, 'Oh! He knew the place very well.' I said, 'He must have walked up past that clump of stringy bark there, and he would go over that heap there — that heap of rock. He would come around on that level track, then he would walk around here and he would come in on the top just here and he would stand where I am standing now. And it was dark,' I said, 'and then he would lean forward and pull the arm, and the body would go down, down, down, and he would hear it.' And I said, 'When he had heard it splash, he would turn away and he would sneak away with his head between his shoulders.' And he said, 'No he didn't — he ran.' And I said, 'Look, you weren't here, so my guess is just as good as yours. I think he sneaked away.' He said, 'He ran, I tell you.' I said, 'How do you know?' And he made this sentence which is like this light. He said, 'I came up here next morning and tracked him, and for a mile his heels never once touched the ground.'*

Now that gives you a picture of a man running in abject terror and horror through the night. Frightened. 'For a mile his heels never once touched the ground.' He could have said to me, 'I tracked him and I could see that he was running,' but that wouldn't have been enough. That wouldn't

* 'When a Man Kills, He Runs', *The Complete Stories of Alan Marshall*, Nelson, page 363.

even have evoked the scene. It wouldn't have been as powerful.

My father used to tell me, too, that every man, every person, knows something better than anyone else in the world, and if you want to educate yourself, if you want to be able to communicate with people, you find out what a man knows that nobody else knows as far as education is concerned, some knowledge he has, and clasp it to you. Learn it. Know it. I used to think of this.

I was driving up a road one day when I saw two workmen picking asphalt. They were digging up the street. And I pulled up and went over to them and I thought—I wonder what these men know. What can I learn from them? And one of them would sink his pick in the asphalt and it used to ring as if it struck iron, and the other man brought his pick down and it went about three inches into the asphalt and they lifted up these great big slabs and the shining tar-covered stones were underneath the slabs. And they levered them back and they fell with a plop on the dull side. And I said, 'It's very hard here,' and he said, 'Well it's hard in some places.' I said, 'But the whole street was laid down at the same time,' and he said, 'Yes, that is right.' 'Well,' I said, 'why do you say it's hard in some places and soft in others?' And he said, 'Well, come along and I will show you. You see now here—just here—I'll bring the pick down here.' He brought the pick down and said, 'This is hard.' Now the pick rang. 'Now,' he said, 'I will show you a soft patch.' So he went a little further and he brought the pick down again and it sank about three inches, and I said, 'How did you know the difference?' 'Well,' he said, 'in this house there are a lot of children, and when the children come out to play at night or in the morning they dance out of that gate and they jump round here in front of the gate and they have worn a sort of depression here, and all their little feet have hammered that asphalt and it becomes as hard as iron. But,' he said, 'in this house an old couple live, and they step out of the gate gently and walk away, and in front of their house the asphalt is soft. That is how I tell the difference.'

The men who arrive at conclusions born of their own reasoning are often uneducated men. They never have newspaper minds, as I call it. They were never brought up like that twelve-year-old boy mentioned in *An American Experience**, who spoke brilliantly to some ambassador for about ten minutes on the political situation in some African country. And after the ambassador had left and the little boy had left, his school-girl daughter told the author that the boy had been repeating two pages of a text book they were studying at school. But he sounded brilliant.

Well, I have often wondered what it is that develops the ability to express yourself instead of repeating the words and conclusions of others. Why is it? Why can the Aborigines, the nomadic ones, the ones who live still their wild life— some years ago there was quite a number—why do they tell stories so beautifully?

I met a Torres Strait Islander on the island of Badu. I stepped off a lugger there and I went for a walk along the beach, and I found myself followed by a group of islanders for no reason that I could imagine. And it seemed to us as if we must be marching to some magnificent spectacle round the next bend. There was going to be a band, or a merry-go-round or something, and bands playing. But I sat down on a log and they all gathered around me in a half-moon. And somebody had told the men on the island—one of the natives—that I tell stories, and they wanted me to tell them a story. But while I was telling this story an old man pushed his way right to the front of the group and sat down looking into my face. And he never moved. He just listened intently. And when I finished he said, 'Good.' And then he said, 'Me, I am a great story-teller—best in all Badu. Very good.' And I asked him if he would tell me a story. And he said, 'Yes,' and he took me away. The crowd just left us and we sat down under a palm tree and I took out my notebook and he said, 'Will I start now?' and I said, 'Yes.' He leaned over and had a look at the page and he said, 'Eh take a new page for me, eh.' I said, 'All right,' and turned over and I took a new page and then he started.†

* By Allan Ashbolt, published by the Australasian Book Society.
† 'See the White Feathers Fall', *The Complete Stories of Alan Marshall*, Nelson, page 232 and *These were my Tribesmen* (chapter 5).

'Long, long time ago, olden day, this was long time ago,' and he told me a story about the men of Tutu, another island, who came over to the island of Badu in the dark in their war canoes and the warriors all wore white birds of paradise plumes in their hair. They were bound round their foreheads and cascaded back over their heads like white water and they landed in the dark. And he said to me, 'Now the story is in the dark. They land, over there,' and I began to realise the wonder of his words and his power to evoke a scene, and you listen entranced to such a speaker. He went on to say that a boy was in the swamp, listening, when these warriors landed and this boy ran to his father to wake him. And the old man said to me, 'His father sleeps. All his fighting gear makes his pillow. His pillow is the stone axe and the spear. And his father sleeps and the boy woke his father up, "Come father. Come war. Come killing." And his father sat up and went with him, and he said to the boy, "Where these people," and the boy said, "Can't you see, Father? See that figure black against the grass. See the head dress white bird feather that is not of the night. See the waving of the white." And the father said, "This is not a white dress feather. This is a white cloud going through the trees." And the boy said, "It is the head dress of the enemy." And the name of this chief was Wyeer.'

And the old man went on. 'The name of the chief in Tutu was Kaigus,' and the old man continued his story. 'Then Wyeer take his spear and his spear was on the ready and he say to his son, "You go home my son," and the boy went, and he alone and Kaigus were standing near a tree. And Wyeer cry out and throw his long spear, and it goes through the river of his back and he falls and dies on the ground.' That sentence, 'the river of his back,' was very beautiful. And he went on to tell me how the men of Badu drove the men of Tutu back through the trees to where their canoes were, and they grabbed two men and cut off their heads, and bound the heads fast with ropes on poles, and the heads they look at the sea, and the bodies come in and go out with the waves. And the Badu men rush into the canoes where they are being taken off by the Tutu warriors, and the old man went on,

'We go into the water up to chest to neck—no grip there. We spear up, and the Tutu men spear down, and the Badu men kill and kill. In the canoes they kill. Everyone die. Everyone killed. No Tutu men live and the Tutu men come in and go out loose in the water, dead in the water, red in the water. All die. It is the end.'

He was a man who had never read a book and I was writing down his dialogue. What made him use such imagery? How did he learn to talk like that?

And amongst the Aborigines in Arnhem Land I was talking to one old man and he was telling me the story of a girl who was a very beautiful woman. And some warrior, some Aborigine, had stolen her and ran away with her. And the relatives pursued him, and killed him, and one of the pursuers, seeing her beauty, ran on further with her. Then more relatives chased them and he was killed. Then one of these pursuers, seeing her beauty fled further, and he too was killed. And then the pursuer fled on and on until many men had died for a hundred miles. But he was telling me, this old man, about how he went out looking for the dead body of one of the men who was killed. And he spoke like this, in a sort of rhythm. He was saying, 'Go, go, go, go, track him from jungle rock to here. Blood all the way. This funny no hawk and crow. They find leaves and tracks all over. They know now. There's a dead body down here. See—some fresh leaf. Not fresh now. He like red leaf now. Dead leaf cover him now. Red leaf cover him now. Then they see him. These three men cry out for that dead body because they find it there. Go get paperbark. Get skinned paperbark and bury him. Come one man. Take this bone, now put him longa bush tree. All right they put him there. It was his dreaming.'*

These stories that were told by these people . . . I think they speak so well and wonder why it is they can express themselves so well. It is because the society in which they live encourages it. It is because their lives circle around communications of this nature. It seems to me that the lives of our children are beginning to circle around TV and I

* *These were my Tribesmen* (chapter 27).

think that what they learn at school is quickly forgotten if it is not practised in the life they lead. These natives lived the life of the stories. They listened and heard them and talked of them continually. And I have always felt that children who express themselves well always come from a home in which they are encouraged to talk. They come from homes in which they are listened to with respect, and if they are brought up to be seen and not heard, as so many children were years ago—and some today, I don't think they can ever learn to communicate with clarity in the way that they want to say.

And communication by talking is only developed by constant practice. I don't think that children can be taught to express themselves orally by listening to the reading of great prose. I think they learn it around the dining table if they have wise parents or parents who hand them that magic leaf each morning. And it seems to me that teachers must have to carry on a continuous battle against against the influence of some parents in order to equip these children for a full and rich life. With other parents, the wise parents, the teachers are partners, but when they look at the child, the pupil, standing in front of them, I am sure they often see the marks of the clutching grass upon them. It sometimes amazes me how magnificently they succeed.

A SENSE OF WONDER

THE beauty of beginnings is that they have nothing to do with age. They happen when we are young; they can happen when we are old.

The question, of course, is what we are beginning. A beginning is worthless if it is not full of promise.

It would be difficult to imagine more inspiring and more promising beginnings than we are experiencing today.* This is so because they are in the nature of praise, praise for achievement. It is a very special praise since it comes from an institution of learning that one feels does not praise without reason.

Thomas Morton, two hundred years ago, commented on the quality of praise when he said:

'Approbation from Sir Hubert Stanley is praise indeed.'

I am tempted now to become a pundit and start giving advice to my fellow graduates based on what is referred to amongst pundits as a 'life-time of experience'. But I remember an entry in one of my notebooks written years ago that now wags a finger at me. It said: 'Advice given in the midst of friends is loathsome.'

What experience has taught me is that age rather than bringing with it tolerance and understanding often leaves one with inflexible judgments and little wisdom. It is not advice from the aged that will help you on your journey through life but lessons learnt from your own experience.

* This address was given when Alan Marshall received the honorary degree of Doctor of Laws at the University of Melbourne 1972.

Life is the great teacher.

There are certain occasions in my life—this is one of them—when I take the opportunity to remind myself that I must never lose something I have carried with me from childhood—the spirit of wonder.

I would like to remind myself of it now; to remind myself that the preservation of the spirit of wonder will keep me young and to warn myself that life without it would lose its magic and I would indeed be old.

We become blasé with the years. Our eyes that once looked at everything for the first time become bored with what they now see and life ceases to have any secrets.

There was a time when the sight of a spider orchid growing in the bush was an emotional experience, an experience that becomes harder to recapture as one grows older.

When I was a child names like 'Early Nancy', 'Black-eyed Susan', 'Eggs-and-Bacon', evoked a feeling of elation. I looked at things with eyes that were receptive to every shape, to every colour. Everything was newly minted for my benefit; everything glowed.

I think it is important to retain this vision throughout life; always to look at things with the eyes of a child while comprehending what you see with the matured mind of an adult.

If we lose this spirit of wonder we have suffered our first death.

For a writer it is extremely important that he views everything as if he were seeing it for the first time. He must never lose touch with the childhood vision, for it is this vision that introduces to his prose the quality that unites him with the reader in a mutual experience.

To illustrate my point.

I remember years ago being friends with an artist and his wife who had a little daughter. She had just reached the stage of learning to walk. This had taken the form of a few uncertain steps within the safety of the house. She had never yet used her legs to carry her into the big world.

One Saturday afternoon they asked me to look after her while they went visiting. We seated ourselves on the edge of the back veranda while I wondered if she would understand a story. Her mother had placed a harness upon her. A strap went round her waist held in place by two straps going over her shoulders. The waist strap had a lead on it with a loop at the end. I was supposed to hold this lead so that she would not be able to wander away from me.

Now all my life I have felt the restrictions of such harness, the harness of restraining authority. It is one of the first restrictions that grown-ups make on our freedom. It wrapped the little girl with frustration. She would totter away the length of the lead, then sit down heavily when she felt the jerk of its control. She would look back at me then, a look of appraisal, a look of resentment. I felt sorry for her and I thought, 'To hell with it.'

I took this yoke from her, this symbol of bondage to grown-ups. I released her. Now she was free to venture out alone into the world of experience.

The back garden in which we sat consisted of an oblong, close-cut lawn surrounded by a high paling fence. Trees and shrubbery concealed the fence. This green palisade contained a lot of rose bushes.

The sun shone strongly here. It was a perfect place to be introduced to adventure.

The little girl was wearing a napkin, so bulky that her legs curved around it like those of a horseman. It seemed to me that she was destined to be bow-legged for ever and I felt sorry for her.

She staggered away from me with arms outstretched like a tight-rope walker, though her steps resembled those of a drunk. Every few yards she sat down heavily upon the ground and the back of her napkin was soon soiled with earth.

She seized these moments of rest to investigate the lawn. Each blade of grass, each tiny pebble, each twig fascinated her. She transferred most things of interest to her mouth. She chewed for a moment reflectively, then spat them out. The world didn't always taste good. When she rose to her feet she did so by placing her hands on the ground and lifting her behind into the air in the way of a rising cow. She would then set out with renewed determination.

She wavered in her walking, veering for no obvious reason, until at last she faced the green shrubbery that sheltered the fence. Here she squatted, her grubby knees forming the apices of two triangles between which she rested with complete comfort.

She sat looking for a long while into the caverns of green opening up in front of her. She reached out a little hand and touched something hidden at arm's length behind leaves. She withdrew her hand and continued looking, her expression one of pleasure.

I wondered what she had discovered, what magical thing gave her that rapt expression. It will be a caterpillar, I thought; maybe it's a hidden flower; perhaps it is a case-moth. I picked up my crutches and swung across the grass until I stood behind her. She looked up at me smiling, then reached out her hand and immersed it in the green. I knelt on the grass beside her and peered into the opening. Her finger was touching a thorn.

It was an arrogant, proud and beautiful thorn. It moved out from the stem of a rose bush in a graceful curve that swept upwards like the prow of a Viking ship. It was smooth and sharp and faultless. It was the first thorn she had ever seen in her life and, looking at it with my face beside hers, I realised it was the first thorn I had ever seen.

THE HORSEMEN OF INNER MONGOLIA

I HAD always wanted to visit Inner Mongolia. In the books of my childhood I had seen pictures of fierce-looking men on shaggy ponies dressed in padded clothes against the cold. The ponies were always pictured galloping across wide grasslands and their riders were obviously pursuing or being pursued. They looked men to whom stirring adventure was a commonplace and skill with horses a necessity.

It was their life as horsemen that appealed to me, their close association with the tireless ponies upon whose backs they seemed to live.

'Horses are shoes,' the Mongolians say, and Malachinfu, a Mongolian writer I met at Huhehot, told me, 'A Mongolian will not walk a hundred yards if he can help it; he will ride.'

But Mongolia was not always associated with horsemen in my childhood mind. There were the Bactrian camels laden with merchandise walking in single file through the arched gateway of a city wall. With my chin on my hands I had gazed at their picture wondering if the wooden peg thrust through each camel's nose hurt it and concluding that their disdainful expression suggested it did not.

A cord was tied to each peg and the other end was tied to the tail of the camel just ahead and in this way they crossed deserts and mountains, swaying like sailing ships as their long, ungainly legs swung forward to each stride. And on their backs were magical things, bound with rope and wrapped in bagging—brocades and silks and fragrant tea. This was Mongolia to me—this and shaggy ponies and the narrow-eyed men with high cheek bones that rode them at a gallop.

So it was that, when as a member of the Australian Cultural Delegation to China, I sat at a table in a palatial hotel at Peking watching Madame Yang Wei-leng writing the requests of each member in her notebook, I decided to ask her if I might visit Inner Mongolia.

Madame Yang Wei-leng was the representative of the Chinese People's Association for Cultural Relations with Foreign Countries and was organising the various tours requested by the delegation.

I always looked at her face with pleasure. It had character and charm. Her eyes twinkled and her smile seemed to anticipate remarks that would develop it into happy laughter. But I was never capable of these remarks and I seemed to be always asking her for some favour: 'When can I see an old man carving ivory?' 'I want to visit a shop where they sell beautiful brocades.' 'I would like to see a panda.'

Now she looked at me across the table waiting for my answer to her question: 'And where would you like to go, Mr Marshall?'

'To Inner Mongolia and see nomads and camels,' I said. 'And I would also like to see a dinosaur's egg, and I want to stand on top of the Great Wall of China.'

When she had written these down I added, 'And I want to go out West as far as I can go.'

Well, these were my requests and, thinking them over afterwards as I sat looking out of the window of my room watching a young Chinese doing breathing exercises on the street below, I concluded they were not suitable requests for a member of a Cultural Delegation, but comforted myself by arguing they were most suitable for me.

So here I was approaching Huhehot, a grey city merging with the landscape as if it had grown out of it without the aid of man.

As we drew in to the station, the long train lost the atmosphere of calm leisure it had carried within it across the mountains and plains; women lifted babies in their arms, men rose to their feet and shouldered huge string bags bulging with their possessions. Between the meshes of these bags I could see colourful things—slippers with bright designs handworked upon them, glimpses of red material, ginger jars . . . a gay umbrella often pierced this collection of foods and on top of them were jammed green vegetables and fruits of purple and yellow. Some men carried bundles dangling at the ends of shoulder poles and some struggled with cases of tan leather protected by dark-green cloth covers. They all crowded into the central corridor and when the train stopped they filed out upon the platform where men paused to search for tickets while wives watched them anxiously.

Two men were waiting for me at the foot of the carriage steps. Fan Sung-hao spoke to them then introduced them—Malachinfu, a Mongolian writer, and Ying Sio-su, a Mongolian painter.

Malachinfu wore grey slacks, a white silk, open-neck shirt and a well-cut sports coat. His companion was dressed in the dark blue uniform popular with many Chinese.

Malachinfu was a restless man with high cheek bones, full lips, a dark complexion and merry eyes. He stepped lightly, sometimes adding unnecessary movements of grace to his walk as if to satisfy some demand of his limbs. I learnt later that for four years he had been a dancer in an Inner Mongolian Singing and Dancing troupe. Before that, as a youth, he had worked for the Eighth Route Army as a 'Carrying Devil', the name given to the young messengers and porters attached to the troops. In 1950 he began writing for *Inner Mongolian Art and Literature*, a periodical published by the Writers' Federation, and his first novel, *People of Kurching Grasslands* was filmed and shown in many countries. He wrote this novel after spending two years among the shepherds of Inner Mongolia, an experience which coloured much of his conversation.

As the car in which we were travelling from the station stopped before the entrance of a huge, modern hotel, I glanced out at its windowed walls and said to him, 'Well, when I was a child I never expected to see a hotel like this in Inner Mongolia.'

'When I was a child I never expected to see one like this either,' he replied.

The suite of rooms into which I was conducted comprised a sitting room furnished with a low table on which rested a teaset of fine china decorated with a design of red horses. In the centre of the table a caddy of carved bamboo contained green tea and beside it were two packets of cigarettes. A large vacuum flask beneath the table contained the hot water for making tea. Large easy chairs surrounded the table, their legs pressed deep into a carpet of a most arresting blue, bordered with pale blue and yellow flowers.

The bedroom adjoining contained a desk with writing paper and ink and a swivel chair of polished wood. The padded bed cover was of blue silk.

The bathroom that opened off the bedroom was a place of gleaming taps and polished porcelain and I wasted no time in getting into the bath. When I had bathed I sat with Malachinfu and Ying Sio-su drinking tea and they asked me what I wished to see in Inner Mongolia.

They listened attentively while I became eloquent on the subject of camels laden with merchandise, Mongolian horsemen and fat-tail sheep, then discussed the matter together.

'It will be two days before we will be able to show you the camels,' they told me and this surprised me since, on our trip from the station, I had seen a string of these animals moving down a narrow street. They would also arrange for me to see a demonstration of horsemanship, they said, and I would most certainly see fat-tail sheep.

I spent the next two days wandering round the city of Huhehot. Like all the Chinese cities I visited it was divided into two sections—the old and the new.

The new section was a place of wide thoroughfares flanked by new brick buildings. Some of these buildings were laced with bamboo scaffolding along which workmen were moving with quick purpose. Others were completed, standing in yet ungardened areas of land with their bright, new interiors quiet like pictures behind a glass of windows.

Some were given life by people sitting before new desks, or moving with sheaves of paper in their hands along corridors, or walking down wide steps to the street. There was a theatre and a school and a building of shops.

In the old section the streets were narrow with shops open to those who passed. Drays with studded wheels loaded with tiles or rocks or bales of hay and pulled by donkeys moved through the people who had spilled from the footpaths on to the roadways where the crowds were thick. Drivers walked beside these drays, long whips in their hands. Sometimes a shaggy pony strained in the shafts while, ahead of it at the end of long rope traces, a tiny donkey added its weight to the pull.

I visited a saddler's shop where saddles hung upon the walls and bridles with broad cheek bands studded with brass were displayed on the counter. The saddles were more like American cowboy saddles than those we use in Australia but the coloured leathers from which they were made, the heavy, brass cloisonné stirrups and their barbaric ornamentation suggested the horsemen of Genghis Khan rather than herdsmen. The tall riding boots displayed on the counter had the turned-up toes I always associated with pictures of Aladdin and indeed, in this dark little shop they had something of the quality of his lamp. They were made from different coloured leathers and shone brightly amid the shadows on the counter.

I was to see such boots upon the feet of galloping horsemen two days later, but first I was taken to see the camels. Malachinfu and Ying Sio-su called for me on a morning when a faint sun was shining palely through a high pall of dust that must have been borne by the cold wind from somewhere far out in the Gobi Desert. The light was eerie, striking no glitters from the polished car in which we travelled through the streets of the old city. We passed through the gateway of the city wall, just such a gateway as, in the pictures of my childhood, was a background for long strings of Bactrian camels laden with merchandise.

Within the wall was a market square and as we approached it I could hear a sound like the breaking of the sea. It was camels I could hear, hundreds of camels. There were old camels and young camels, baby camels that walked awkwardly, that tottered and stumbled on untrained legs. There were ancient camels with disdainful expressions and vicious tempers and some that seemed mild and tranquil. I jumped from the car and fairly bathed in camels. Valiant camel drivers wearing skull caps and blue coats and trousers jumped between me and camels that would have taken my arm off with one snap, so I was told.

The drivers were happy laughing men. They were amused at my interest in things that were commonplace to them — the pegs in the nostril of each camel, the cords that tied each beast to the tail of the one in front, the two humps on their backs and the sacking-covered bundles they bore. Here was the merchandise I had wanted to see. I was sure that if I took my pocket knife and cut a hole in this sacking I would uncover rich brocades and silks, fragrant tea and ivories carved by masters. There would be peacock feathers and embroidered gowns and bangles of gold. Through Mr Fan Sung-hao I asked one of the drivers what his camel was carrying beneath the sack wrappings and he said, 'Old sticks.'

As I stood looking at this huge mob of camels with their drivers moving amongst them, all gathered there for my benefit, I wondered where they had all been scattered two days before. I suddenly had a picture of them then, some threading their way through passes in hills, some crossing desert stretches, some watering their beasts at lonely rivers, and I imagined word passing from one to another, 'Come to Huhehot flat out; an Australian wants to look at camels. And don't forget to load them with merchandise!'

Then whips would be raised and men would shout commands and camels would bray protestingly and from East and West and North and South strings of camels swathed in dust would race for this grey city; upon their backs men in skull caps would rock and sway while they pondered on the peculiarities of Australians.

How I loved these drivers!

'I want to take a movie picture of the camels walking,' I told them and they leapt upon the camels' back and that huge mob of animals began to unravel itself like a ball of wool. They turned and twisted, walked in and out and around, each camel tied to the tail of the one in front of it. They passed me in single file where I stood like a general taking the salute, and as they passed the drivers smiled and waved. The thick masses of brown hair hanging from the camels' front legs and shoulders flopped against the animals as they swayed past. I turned and watched them moving away, their thin, long back legs seeming frail and out of proportion to the weight and strength of the rest of their bodies.

I saw the horsemen next day. On a flat plain beyond the city I sat at a cloth-covered table on which were mugs of tea and cigarettes. With me were some officials and Malachinfu. There was a cold wind coming from the mountains behind us and Malachinfu wrapped his blue overcoat around me. Surrounding the flat area in front of me a large crowd of people had gathered. They seemed infected with pleasurable excitement like an Australian rodeo crowd and when the horsemen appeared at one end of the field they cheered them.

A tall Mongolian wearing a long purple gown tied with a red sash had taken up his place in the centre of the field and with a shout the horsemen galloped towards him, each pony at its top. They passed him and swerved away, each horseman placing one foot upon the saddle and saluting as he passed. Each feat of horsemanship that followed was executed as the group of riders galloped past this man.

There were ten horsemen and they began each gallop from the far end of the field, the ponies gaining speed with each bound of their powerful bodies. They were stocky, thickset ponies with large, horselike heads.

'They all seem to have large heads,' I said to one of the officials.

'Large heads!' he repeated in surprise.

'Yes,' I said, 'they seem too large in proportion to their bodies.'

'Too large?' he questioned as if he had not heard rightly.

'Yes,' I said—rather smugly, I'm afraid—'in Australia the ponies' heads are much smaller.'

He recovered himself, swallowed, then said sharply, 'In Australia the ponies' heads are much too small.'

And I think he was right.

The ponies were tireless, they never flagged in their furious galloping. Men stood upright upon their backs, their arms extended each side of them like wings. They rode the wind across that plain. The riders stood upon their heads on the saddles, their toes pointing skywards like ballet dancers. They leapt from side to side of galloping ponies, stood on each other's shoulders, made pyramids of men upon groups of ponies galloping side by side. With flashing sabres they slashed through small branches hanging from poles; they sat upon the ponies' rumps, their legs brushed by streaming tails as they fired repeating rifles at imaginary pursuers. The ponies, galloping with free bridles, never faltered in their stride. Then around the riders would whirl and puffs of smoke would come from the barrels resting between the ponies' ears. They shot to the right, the left, into the air. Acrobatic riders spun on poles connecting two running ponies. Ponies, apparently riderless, would speed past in groups and suddenly men would rise from their sides, salute and disappear again.

Ponies sprang and wheeled and propped and reared skyward with the smoke of rifles around their heads. The red silk jackets of the riders fluttered in the wind. Men shouted from amid swirls of dust that divided and revealed riders reefing on the reins while the ponies with lifted heads and open mouths came round in tight propping turns.

'Mr Marshall,' said the official sitting next to me, 'can you suggest any way in which we can improve this spectacle?'

CHEN CHU HUA AND THE
THIRTY SACKS OF RICE

CHEN Chu Hua was born at Ning Po, a village eleven hours journey by boat from Shanghai. She was a pretty little girl who viewed the world into which she was born with excitement and wonder. Her parents were poor peasants but in her childhood the burden of debt under which they laboured did not cloud her happiness or trouble her with dark forebodings.

She was a child. The sun shone only for her, the flowers of spring came to carpet the earth upon which she walked, the trees were her friends; life was a wonderful adventure.

The house in which she lived with her parents was quite close to the Landlord's home, a large house surrounded by a garden. She was not supposed to enter this garden but sometimes, with other children, she would sneak in to look at the flowers or to watch the goldfish swimming in their lily-covered pool. She loved the goldfish. She would squat with her little knees beneath her chin and look down at them entranced. They affected her like music.

The children were not afraid of the Landlord. He was old and wrinkled, and sat crouched in his room amid the smoke of smouldering opium. Sometimes his attendant chased the children but they ran faster than he and he could not catch them. Then the attendant would shout and throw stones at them and they would run from the garden afraid.

When Chen Chu Hua was a little older she began saving cigarette cards and marbles. These were her treasures, the things with which she played when she was lonely. She could not read the writing on the cards or understand the story behind some of the pictures for she never went to school but sometimes she looked for a long time at the writing as if by concentration she could solve its meaning. The children of the Landlord could read and write but they had been taught these things. You could not learn to read by looking intently at printed words, though she often wished that this was so.

She never saw a pencil till she was twelve. At this age she began helping her parents in the fields of the Landlord. Now with the knowledge of her parents' condition life resolved itself into two states—debt was worry and trouble; freedom from debt was happiness. To her it was just as simple as that. She had no dreams of marriage with some man she loved, some home of her own gladdened by the laughter of her children. Her mind was occupied with looking ahead to that bright time when her parents would be free of debt. In her restricted world a happy life for her would only begin when her parents were free of the Landlord's power. Until this was accomplished there was no future for her worthy of her striving.

When she was sixteen their poverty was extreme. For a few weeks her parents were silent in her presence, their faces tight with worry. Then her father told her: 'We do not earn enough to buy our food,' he said. 'We are never free of hunger. The interest on our debt to the Landlord is increasing every month. He keeps pressing us for payment and we cannot pay. You must marry the Landlord's son. He wants you and if you marry him his father will give us time to pay. If you do not do this we are lost.'

'When do you wish me to marry him?' she asked.

'Tomorrow,' he said.

When Chen Chu Hua, now a woman of thirty-one, told me this I was sitting beside her on a divan in the assembly room of the Women's Reformation House at Shanghai.

It was morning and outside I could hear a woman singing. Beyond the window flowers made a blazing patch of colour in an open courtyard. On my left, Wang Jo-von, a Shanghai writer and editor-in-chief of the *Literary Journal Monthly*, leant back in his chair, a neglected cigarette hanging loosely between his fingers, his sensitive face touched with compassion as he listened to her words. On my right the interpreter, Mr Fan Sung-hao, never took his eyes from her face. In front of me, across the table upon which glasses of green tea were gently steaming, sat the head of this collection of buildings with its hospital, recreation hall, workshops and reading rooms. Her face was a book upon which I could read the changing moods of Chen Chu Hua's story, the sadness, the happiness, the horror that lay behind the words she spoke so quietly.

She was telling me the story of her life, why she was now an inmate of this home instead of a housewife in the village of Ning Po.

She had entered the assembly room smiling shyly at me, had shaken my hand, and sat beside me with dignity. She spoke rapidly, with feeling, with expressive gestures. She had a kindly face that bore a gentle expression when she paused to allow Mr Fan to interpret her words.

'Tomorrow!' she had said, and suddenly her face crumpled a little and tears trickled down her cheeks and fell upon the sleeves of her blue jacket.

'Tomorrow!' and it must have all come back to her, all the horror of it. She was only sixteen and the Landlord's son was forty-one. He had had two wives. One had died and the other had run away. Now her. And he smoked opium like his father. He wanted an attendant, her parents said. She would prepare the opium, strike the match, bring his slippers, his cups of tea.

. . . She would lie beside him at night, staring into the dark. And for this the Landlord would not press her father for money.

Her tears fell on her blue jacket. I stroked her shoulder with my hand. She stopped and looked at me, waiting for me to speak.

'So you married him?'

'Yes.'

'Was he cruel to you?'

'He was always scolding, always bad-tempered. But not when he was smoking opium. He told me he smoked opium

because his father told him to. He said his father said to him,
"If you are a good son you must always keep the property of
your forefathers. To do this you must smoke so that you will
never be tempted to leave your home. This is the only way to
make you contented at home." That was why he began
smoking opium,' she said.

'Now tell me what happened to you after your marriage?' I
asked her.

She continued her story.

The home to which her husband took her was close to the
small village hotel in which travellers, passing through the
village, often stayed the night. An old woman took a room
there. She made friends with Chen Chu Hua and began
visiting her when Chen Chu Hua's husband was away. The
lonely little wife only saw friendship in the hard, calculating
eyes of this evil woman.

'You are young and beautiful,' this old woman told her.
'Why do you go on living with this old man you do not love?
I could get you work in a factory at Shanghai and you would
be happy there.'

One morning she rose before dawn and left the house. She
had told her husband she was going to feed the pigs but she
met the old woman and together they boarded the river
steamer as it was about to leave for Shanghai. Her only
possessions were the clothes she wore.

When they reached Shanghai the old woman took her to a
house where she was met by another woman who eyed her
appraisingly. In the morning a document was placed before
her upon which she was asked to place her thumb print.

'It is a contract to work in a factory,' they told her, so she
pressed her ink-smeared thumb upon it, feeling that this was
the beginning of a new and happy life for her.

The woman who owned the house then locked her in a
room and paid thirty sacks of rice to the old woman who had
brought her from Ning Po. The thirty sacks of rice was the
price the old woman received for having sold Chen Chu
Hua to a brothel.

The days that followed were days of horror and despair
for Chen Chu Hua. She refused to receive the guests, those

men who for fifty cents paid to the Madam were entitled to spend two hours with her. The other inmates of this terrible house, peasant girls who, like her, had been lured there by lies, told her to go to the police even though they knew this would be of little use. The Madam herself took her to the police station; to the police she had already paid to protect her interests.

The police photographed Chen Chu Hua and filed her picture with those of other prostitutes so that if she tried to escape she would be recognised by the police and brought back to the Madam. They looked at her thumb print upon the contract and told her that she now belonged to the Madam and would have to return to the brothel.

But she still refused to receive the guests. The Madam held her weakened body upon a bed, bound a padded cover about her face so that her cries would not disturb the patrons, then proceeded to twist and pinch her body until it became one huge and throbbing bruise. The Madam did not touch her face. It was too valuable. Its beauty was the bait to lure the men into her house. She starved Chen Chu Hua, withholding food from her. She tortured her again. Chen Chu Hua began receiving guests, her mind dulled with pain and weakness.

The girls called each other 'sister'. They were all young, at that age when the bloom of youth should have been upon them. Now with loathsome disease creeping through their bodies they became old when they were young. They died in suffering and filth when life should have just been beginning for them.

When in their early twenties, when their poor, contaminated bodies no longer attracted guests, the Madam murdered them. Chen Chu Hua had witnessed three such murders. The first, a girl of nineteen, had been brought to the brothel when she was twelve. At fourteen she was receiving guests. Disease moved swiftly through her. At nineteen the Madam decided it would cost more to have her cured than it would to buy a new girl, so she locked her in an upstairs room and left her alone to die of starvation and sickness.

The second sister Chen Chu Hua saw murdered was only

eighteen when she died. She was laying upon her bed in the last extremity of the disease from which they all suffered. She would earn no more money for the Madam, but she was still eating food. The Madam came in and looked down on her as she lay with closed eyes breathing heavily. What use was she now! This hideous trader in women's bodies seized the padded bed cover and holding it tightly over the young girl's face, she smothered her.

The third murder witnessed by Chen Chu Hua was that of a young peasant girl who lay in a small room on the third floor in the midst of premature labour. The Madam, pretending to help her to another room, suddenly hurled her from the top of the stairs so that she fell screaming for two flights before she was silenced in a huddled heap on the distant landing with a new born baby on the floor beside her. All the sisters saw this. They screamed hysterically. They ran from room to room with loud cries like animals. The Madam shouted back. She locked them all in their respective rooms and left them there for two days without food until they were willing to receive the guests once more.

Hurling girls from the top of the stairs was Madam's favourite method of getting rid of her unprofitable girls. She killed several in this way. After Chen Chu Hua told me this she was trembling. She clasped and unclasped her hands and I waited a little while until she was calm again.

'I can't understand why you did not run away,' I said to her.

'It was impossible to escape,' she said. 'Whenever Madam went out she locked us in the building. The windows were barred with iron. Even if we did get out we had no money and nowhere to go. Those who tried were always brought back by the police. Madam paid them well.'

'Was it impossible for you to save some money?' I asked her. 'Didn't some of the men give you gifts of money besides what they paid the Madam?'

'The Madam kept all the money,' Chen Chu Hua explained. 'There was a hole in the wall of every room and Madam watched us through these holes. If we received a gift of money she knew and we had to give it to her.'

There were twenty-four sisters in the brothel in which Chen Chu Hua was a prisoner. None of them had ever managed to escape, though many had tried. Death was their only escape. When one died, another girl was brought by the Madam to take her place. They lived there a few short years then died in the agony of disease or were murdered as they lay weak in their beds. None of them could read or write. They knew nothing of the world outside the walls of the brothel in which they were imprisoned. They knew nothing of human kindness or compassion. They only knew the beast in men.

Then came Liberation. Brothels were declared illegal, the Madams were arrested and the sisters were taken to Reformation Houses to begin the education that was to fit them for the normal life of decent people. The Madam who owned Chen Chu Hua had told the sisters that the Army of Liberation intended sending them all to the Front where they would be shot. Chen Chu Hua believed this and after the Madam was arrested and Chen Chu Hua was taken to the Reformation House she refused to accept the cadres there as friends. She screamed at the one allotted to her, spat on her, threw cups at her. But the cadre was patient. It was her task to teach this poor girl that another life was opening up for her, a life in which she could work like other girls, a world in which she could read and write, hear great music, learn to talk and mix with people who had no intention of exploiting her. Doctors would cure her of the disease from which she suffered, she would be given clothes, good food, and opportunities to develop any talents she possessed. At last she believed and began the long journey back to health and decency.

As she finished her story she smiled at me in happiness. She took her notebook and pen from my hand and wrote her name for me to see. She can write a thousand characters, she told me, and she can read. Never again will she have to gaze intently at the words on the back of cigarette cards hoping that their meaning will be magically revealed to her. Magic has already entered her life. Her sickness is cured. She is now strong and healthy and in a few weeks will be going out into the world of good people to some job allotted to her. There are seven hundred and eighty women like her in this lovely house. They got tea for me, brought chairs for me to sit on, shook my hand and laughed at my jokes. Their dark and terrible past will have no place in their future. A miracle has happened to them. They have been recreated.

I said goodbye to Chen Chu Hua amid the flowers in the courtyard. She held my hand, looking at me with an intent seriousness as if she wished to impress some important truth upon me.

'If Liberation had been delayed only one year, I would be dead now,' she said. Then she relaxed and smiled as she added, 'I look on the People's Government as my parents now; they will look after me.'

DEATH COMES TO A MAMMOTH

MAYBE my interest in mammoths goes back to Arthur Mee. He was the editor of *The Children's Encyclopaedia*, *The Children's Newspaper*, and *My Magazine* when I was a child. The encyclopaedia appeared as a monthly magazine in those days and I was one of his most enthusiastic readers.

The illustrations that accompanied his articles on prehistoric animals established their appearance permanently in my mind and when, in the Leningrad Museum, I actually saw a mammoth that had been discovered frozen in the permafrost of Siberia, some minor differences in formation between it and Arthur Mee's conception of the animal destroyed my faith in him as an authority.

The Leningrad mammoth, preserved for 30,000 years beneath the landslide of a Siberian river gorge, had a head, the top of which rose in helmet fashion above the massive forehead. Arthur Mee slipped badly in his picture of a mammoth's head. But on looking back over a few old copies of his magazine I think the less said about his mistakes, the better.

I had not reached the stage of seeing an entire mammoth without a prior introduction to some of its parts.

The Russians are the kindest and most thoughtful of hosts and my interest in mammoths resulted in me meeting those professors attached to the Institute of Palaeontology in Moscow, in which city I stayed for a few weeks prior to visiting Leningrad. I found that the Soviet scientist does not sit on some elevated position out of reach of laymen like myself but meets you on terms that seem to lift you to his level of knowledge. Your ignorance in his particular field is not then a burden and you feel free to seek information more ponderous men might regard as trivial.

'I would like to own the hair of a mammoth,' I told one of the institute's professors. 'Bones do not evoke a living thing; hair does.'

He considered this, then said, 'We can certainly get you the hair of a mammoth. If you had asked for a whole mammoth it would be much more difficult.'

A week later a member of the Soviet-Australia Friendship Society handed me an envelope containing two black hairs from the tail of a mammoth. They were about six inches long; like horse hair but much coarser.

The note accompanying them stated they were from 'MAMMUTHUS PRIMIGENIUS BLUM' and were a present from Professor Dr C. C. Flarov, Chief, Palaeontological Museum, Academy of Science of USSR.

Professor Flarov was not only a famous palaeontologist but a gifted artist as well. His paintings of prehistoric animals are known all over the world and illustrate many books on the subject. They have established the outward appearance of animals no human being has ever seen since they lived many millions of years before man appeared on the Earth. The pictures of these animals are not now the fantasies of unrestrained imaginations but are based on a science which is going deeper and deeper into the Earth's past. Hide and colour and behaviour are not now described from imagination but from evidence palaeontologists are continually unearthing.

Arthur Mee said mammoths were covered with a thick coat of reddish hair, a statement I would have doubted after his mistake about their heads, but a week after receiving the two tail hairs, a doctor of biology I had met gave me an envelope containing a big tuft of reddish hair from the side of a mammoth.

I had now progressed from the tail halfway to the head as far as evidence of a mammoth's existence was concerned and would have been content to take the necessity of a head for granted, but a fortnight later the same biologist came climbing the stairs to my hotel room carrying a brief-case which he lowered to the floor with an expression of relief. He sat on a chair then opened the case and took out a brown paper parcel which he unwrapped with care while my daughter and I watched him. He placed the object he uncovered on the floor between us.

'A mammoth's tooth,' he said and he said it in the same tone one would have said 'a pound of butter'.

'It is a back tooth from the right side of the lower jaw,' he went on. 'It is estimated to be almost 30,000 years old and came from a mammoth that died in the prime of life—about forty-five years old, I would say.'

He made this mammoth immediate and real. The tooth ceased to suggest a species of animal that once existed in totality, a species I saw as an abstraction labelled 'Mammoth' in which individual animals had no part, but evoked a picture of one doomed mammoth that died in its prime with the file-like serrations on its tooth's surface still unworn.

I wanted to know more about this one splendid mammoth that in the remote past had cheated utter annihilation by communicating to me its identity and its death across the silence of 30,000 years.

'Was it a male or a female?' I asked.

'A male.'

Well, it was a male. It had been covered in coarse, reddish hair that at times must have been frozen into a sheath upon it when the winter cold went down to 30 degrees below and the air crackled and the midday sun moved no more than its own height above the horizon.

'Where was it found?'

'Near the mouth of the Neva.'

'What would I have seen had I been there?'

'The wide tundra, mosses and lichens and dwarf shrubs, the high banks of the Neva where huge ice blocks grind together in the spring.'

'It would not be alone, of course.'

'No. They lived in herds. A number of them were trapped there. Some must have broken through the ice into deep bogs.'

'How it must have struggled,' I said. 'This mammoth, this male mammoth . . . The others would move away.'

'Yes,' he said, then added. 'Maybe a female waited for a little while beside the place.'

I held the tooth in my hands. It weighed 4½ pounds, was ten inches long and three inches wide. It must have stood about three inches above the flesh of the jaw when the mammoth lived.

I held it high.

'Imagine carrying that around in your mouth,' I said.

I don't think the doctor tried to imagine it.

I saw the mammoth as a whole in Leningrad where in the Palaeontological section of the museum I was greeted by a professor whose named ended in 'ski', I think. I should have written it down, but I didn't.

He was a man whose life was devoted to a study of pre-historic animals. He smiled a lot, sometimes at me and sometimes with me, and was the type of man who responds with pleasure to a genuine interest in his work.

'Tell me exactly what you want to see,' he said.

'I want to see the mammoth your scientists found frozen on the banks of the Berezovka River,' I said. 'I want to see its actual flesh and the lump of food that was taken from its mouth. I want to be shown exactly how it was found and discuss how it came to break its back. I'd like to see the break. I want to know how much of its trunk wolves had eaten. I'd like to be told what mammoth tastes like. I understand one of your scientists ate a piece.'

'Where did you obtain all this information?' he asked in surprise.

'From the *Children's Magazine*,' I told him.

'Oh!' he said, and I don't blame him.

He took me down long rooms to a place where skeletons, towering to the roof, snarled down at me with triangular teeth sharp as knives, to where there were gigantic skulls bearing horns, tusks, bony protuberances. They stared at me with their eye hollows from behind thick glass, older by millions of years than my mammoth, an animal highly civilised by their reptilian standards.

'There is the material taken from the mammoth's mouth,' said the professor, pointing to a large jar in which a tangled lump of twigs and stems had been preserved.

Some of the stems were as thick as a pencil. Some were flattened and marked by the huge teeth that had begun to grind them.

'What shrub was it eating?' I asked.

'Dwarf birch.'

He pointed to another jar.

'This is its flesh, fatty tissue.'

The flesh was coarse and stringy like that of an old bull.

'Is it true that a scientist ate a piece of it?'

'Yes,' he said, 'the taste was most unpleasant.'

(A few weeks later Boris Polavoi, a famous Soviet writer, told me that there was an old trapper in Bratsk, Siberia, who had eaten mammoth flesh when he found himself short of food. Polavoi asked him what it tasted like, and he said, 'Abominable. I don't like talking about it. I've never tasted anything more disgusting or horrible in all my life.')

'Yet men of that time ate them,' I said to the professor. 'Their broken bones have been found in caves used by Magdalenian hunters.'

'The meat would be fresh then,' he said.

He took me to a huge glass case, the size of a small room, in which the Berezovka mammoth rested. It was mounted exactly as it had been found, buried deep beneath the frozen banks of the river after great floods had washed the earth away and released it from the long darkness of 30,000 years into the sunshine of today.

It was sitting on its haunches, its hind legs doubled beneath it. Its front legs were straightened in a position of arrested movement, lifting the forepart of its body some distance above the ground. It had died in a squatting position. Though larger than an elephant its ears were much smaller. ('Big ears would have frozen in the cold,' said the professor.) Its trunk was much thicker than that of an elephant and its tusks instead of projecting in an upward curve extended in front of it as if they were beginning a spiral, the points converging on each other.

It had a retreating forehead and a domed head. The hair that covered it was long, thick, coarse and red in colour.

Well, this was a mammoth! What amazed me as I looked at it was how accurately the artists of stone age tribes had engraved pictures of it on ornaments of bone, horn and ivory discovered in caves they had frequented.

I remember a superb picture of a charging mammoth engraved by a Magdalenian craftsman on bone, a photograph of which I had hanging in my room in Australia. The cave of the Combarelles and that of Bernifal have wall engravings of mammoths. There were vivid polychrome cave paintings of the animals by the Magdalenians who lived in Spain and France.

I wondered whether this mammoth had ever seen a man. A human skeleton 30,000 years old had been found at Vladimir, 120 miles north-west of Moscow. It was decorated with beads and bracelets of mammoth ivory. He must have killed mammoths.

The only evidence that man had hunted and killed the mammoth is to be found in engravings on mammoth bones and reindeer antlers many of which were discovered near Kursk in the USSR.

These late palaeolithic hunter-artists lived in large communities. Some of their engravings illustrate the type of trap they used — pits and log-falls — but finally the mammoth died from spears and the battering from weapons of stone.

These hunters must have found it easier to kill young mammoths they could cut off from the herd since the bones of mammoths not fully grown litter their buried encampments. Amongst the bones of the young were often the bones of very old animals that, defenceless from age, had been slain in solitary places where they had been deserted by the herd. The very young and the very old were their victims.

When these hunters died they were laid in the earth and the shoulder blades of mammoths were placed over them as if furnishing a protection. Several graves with the bodies thus protected have been found. One was that of a woman about forty-five. She lay doubled up beneath the huge, flat bone.

Some of their dwellings were built of mammoth bones and these have been unearthed just as they were when the hunters lived in them.

These brave hunters followed the mammoths. In the bleak winters herds of these huge beasts lumbered like galleons across snow seas followed by the Magdalenians. There must have been a great feasting when a beast was killed. And a weeping sometimes, too. Hunters would die on the great tusks of these animals when enraged by pain they turned upon them.

'How did this mammoth die?' I asked the professor. 'Wasn't its back broken?'

'Yes, it was,' he said. 'We think it must have been grazing on the edge of a cliff formed by a high bank of the Berezovka River. The edge of the cliff must have broken away hurling the mammoth hundreds of feet below where it broke its back on the rocks. Hundreds of tons of earth would cover it— frozen earth. It would die instantaneously.'

'I don't believe it did,' I said. 'I believe it struggled. That mammoth didn't die instantaneously.'

I watched his wonderful smile emerge as he considered this.

'We believe it died instantaneously,' he said. 'If it hadn't it would have swallowed that mouthful of food.'

'Look,' I said. 'When a horse gets a fright it clenches its teeth. It takes the bit in its teeth, as they say. They do it when in pain, too. I've watched horses in acute pain. They hold their breath and clench their teeth. That's what this mammoth did. It was frightened as it fell. It didn't land on its back. If it had it could never have got into the position in which you found it. It landed upright. A huge rock following it down broke its back. It went down, its hindquarters paralysed. Then it made one desperate effort to rise. It put its front legs in the position a horse does when it's rising. Then the earth came over it, surged under its forequarters. It was held in this position and that's how you found it.'

'Hm!' said the professor.

'It would be making south to escape the cold,' I said, creating the scene for my own benefit.

'We believe it was making north,' said the professor. 'Mammoths like the cold. It was after the last glaciation and the ice would be retreating.'

'Well, all right,' I said, feeling annoyed with Arthur Mee. 'It was making north. Now tell me, where was its back broken?'

He pointed to the next case.

'There's its skeleton.'

'But where's its broken spine?' I asked, examining the skeleton where every bone was as it was in life.

'We mended it with plaster,' explained the professor lamely.

'You shouldn't have done that!' I exclaimed. 'It spoils it.'

'You see,' said the professor, 'you are interested in the story; we are interested in the animal.'

'An understanding of the one is necessary for an understanding of the other,' I argued.

He laughed and took hold of my arm for a moment in a gesture of friendliness.

'I can see you love horses,' he said. 'Would you like to see Peter the Great's horse?'

HORSES AND POETS OF ABKHAZIA

I HAD to shout at this man so he could hear me. The wind seemed to be making a terrific noise as it swept over the car in a triumphant curve. He was a dark man with a flowing moustache and black eyes that seemed to express amusement whenever he looked at me. I had met a drover like him near Wilcannia: you always suspect they are going to pull your leg.

This man was a taxi driver. He could speak English, too. He was an unusual man. A framed photograph of his ten-year-old daughter was hanging on the instrument panel in front of him and he looked at it quite often. When he looked at it he smiled, then he would glance at me and raise his hand in the air and waggle his fingers in a display of pride. His daughter was very clever, he said. She smiled at me from the photograph and I liked her.

It was late afternoon in summer and we had not long left Sukhumi, the capital of Abkhazia, which is part of the Georgian Republic in southern USSR. Sukhumi is on the eastern shores of the Black Sea and has a history dating back to the first century BC when it was under Roman rule. The Turks captured it in the second half of the fifteenth century and built a fortress there—Sukhum-Kale—the ruins of which can be seen today.

Now it is a modern city with wide streets shaded by our gum trees, a health resort with streaming white sunlight that tans the bodies of bikini-clad women holidaying on its beaches.

The taxi driver told me it averages 200 sunny days a year. Maybe so. He was brown enough. It can get cold there though. I noticed that many of the avenues of gums (Tasmanian blue gums, they were) appeared as if a bush fire had passed through them. Their leaves were brown and withered though green suckers were already pushing their way through the cracked bark.

The winter was very cold,' the taxi driver told me. 'It went down to 20 degrees below. It killed all the eucalypts but most of them will become green again.'

I was glad of that. I hated to think of a gum tree dying beside the Black Sea; so far away from Australia, it seemed.

We were driving through the Caucasian Mountains on our way to some remote village where Abkhazian and Georgian poets were to give a reading of their work.

I kept thinking about this and I visualised a building something like a Mechanics Institute of our country towns where there was a platform and an old piano and a floor covered with sawdust to preserve it for dancing. There will be about half a dozen there, I thought, and I won't be able to pronounce their names. I had a momentary feeling of depression but I found it impossible to retain it.

At every hairpin bend, and they were continuous, the tyres of the taxi gave a horrible screech, and I became concerned with self-preservation. My daughter and an interpreter were sitting in the back seat and they kept sliding from one side of the seat to the other with expressions that seemed to suggest their concerted movement was normal. As they slid they looked at the scenery. Their attitude seemed to me a reflection on my character. I put a calm expression on my face but first of all made an explanation to the driver.

'I always associate the scream of tyres with a loud bang and a body by the side of the road with blood on its face,' I said.

He looked at me in astonishment as if I had suddenly revealed depths of depravity in myself.

I became convinced I had. I hurriedly changed the subject.

'Are many cows killed on this roadway?' I shouted.

I asked this because he was missing cows by a finer margin than anything else.

'No,' he replied. 'Cows are predictable. They either stand without moving or move very slowly. In both cases you can avoid them. People,' he continued as we passed under the curve of a man with upraised arms in the graceful posture of a bull-fighter avoiding a bull,' are not predictable. One never knows which way they will leap. Missing them demands judgment.'

In Abkhazia, cows, donkeys, geese and goats share the roads equally with people. Men and women walk home in strings from the fields often carrying bundles of hay or firewood on their heads. Yellow cows stand chewing their cud, their long-lashed eyes half-closed, their lifted heads projecting over the narrow roadway. They turn their heads away from the cars when they hear them and often I found myself looking through the side window into the single eye of a cow, unafraid, a few inches away from me.

Sitting in the seat that in Australia is always occupied by the driver is an unnerving experience for a while. Head-on collisions appear imminent. The heads of horses are wrenched to one side by peasant drivers holding the reins from the seats of low wagons laden with hay. Approaching cars seem to swerve in the wrong direction.

The most disdainful users of the roads are the geese and the goats. Geese cluster round a gander by the side of a road waiting for his lead across. When he steps out on to the roadway with his head held high and the loose skin between his legs swinging they follow him blindly, in single file. The last goose to cross is the one who has to make the desperate, flapping hop to safety on the other side.

Goats never alter their step. A blaring horn is unheard, the screech of brakes only makes them look more contemptuous.

Donkeys, flicking their tails with annoyance, move aside at the last moment.

They all retain their dignity—the geese, the donkeys, the cows and the goats. Only human beings make ungainly leaps or give you momentary glimpses of wide open, glazed eyes just beyond the window.

But away from the villages the people become fewer. Deep

in the mountains the late afternoon sun seemed to kindle a light in all the trees on the western slopes of the hills. A radiant green coloured the very air. There was no wind, no touch of mountain cold in the passes. We wound through them and below us were undulating hills patched with forest, fields and sheep with floppy ears and black faces, little houses in nests of trees and a tremendous feeling of space purified by sunlight.

We came to the village where the poets were to meet. There was no Mechanics Institute, only a clump of huge feathery-leafed trees—acacias, I think they were—beneath which stood a crowd of people. There must have been over 300 men, women and children standing there. They had gathered themselves into the shape of a crescent and were facing a long table covered with a green cloth. Men were sitting at this table, poets—the poets of Abkhazia.

I sat with them and I looked at the people. In the front row were a number of old men sitting on chairs. Behind them were the people—men wearing fez-like hats of astrakhan, women holding babies, children in embroidered frocks, girls with long black hair, their hands on the arms of boys proud with possession. They awaited the poets, their faces touched with some anticipation of beauty yet to come.

But it was the old men in the front row who held my attention. I knew them well. I had met them in my childhood picture books. These were the brave horsemen of Abkhazia, men who in pictures stained by sticky fingers, tattered by use, fought with sword and dagger from the backs of rearing horses against a background of mosque and minaret, and there was the dust of hooves and wild yells that only I could hear.

The clothes of the old men were the same as those in these faded pictures. They wore lamb-skin hats, long black cloaks, riding trousers and knee-high boots of black leather. Around their waists were leather belts from which hung the silver-decorated scabbards of daggers, the chased hilts of which I could see projecting from the blade's cover.

They had dark eyes and sweeping white moustaches. Their noses were strong and prominent. There was a fierce pride in their glance—pride and dignity and courage. Ah, that spirit that held their old bodies erect in the chairs.

The poets read their poems, some from books in which the printed words looked like embroidery, some from memory.

They did not read them as one would in drawing-rooms but as one would read them under the sky standing on the earth one loved. They gestured, raised proclaiming hands aloft, gave their strong voices to the people as one would give water to the thirsty.

I kept thinking of a painting that once had impressed me. It was of Rouget de Lisle singing the Marseillaise after he had first composed it. He had one hand aloft, the other on his chest and those who were listening to him were leaning forward entranced.

The reading stopped, the applause died away, the old men rose from their chairs and walked off amongst the trees. I wondered where they were going.

The people moved across the grassy slope that stretched back from the trees. They formed a corridor about seventy-five yards long. The two walls of people were separated by about ten yards. The table at which I sat was at one end of the corridor, a little to the side. I was puzzled. I looked down between the two rows of people and wondered what it had to do with the reading of poetry.

Suddenly into the open space near the table rode the old men. Their prancing horses, with nostrils flaring, champed the bits while flecks of foam drifted from their mouths. They were fine-boned horses with delicately moulded heads and large eyes. They were bays and greys and blacks. They held their narrow tails well away from their rumps in the manner of Arabs and tossed their heads reefing at the bits, eager to be away. They centred their back hooves beneath them, then reared with arched necks, striking at the air before landing to continue their nervous dancing.

The old men sat loosely upon them, giving to every change of movement, but the thin, bony hands that gripped every rein were as inflexible as steel. They wore cruel spurs, but the flanks of their horses were unmarked. They held their feet forward, the spurs out and down. The thick whips they carried were never used to strike their horses. They cracked them like Australian stockmen, the horses quivering to every report. They shouted commands to their horses who with ears turned backward responded to each order in sudden passions of movement.

Each man galloped the length of the corridor and back in a display of horsemanship. The quickness of the get-away, the speed of the turn and the abruptness of the stop were the factors that established the skill of the riders.

They began with a shout. The horses, back on their haunches, leaped forward at the slackened rein. The old men stood up in the stirrups, the wind of their speed fluttering their white moustaches against their cheeks. At the end of the lane each horse came round in one fierce movement, scattering tufts of grass and soil torn loose by their polished hooves.

In the last stretch the old men seemed to lift the horses beneath them. Their eagle-faces rose above the heads of the horses as they thundered towards my table. Then the reef and the rear, the stop and the prancing and the sound of snorting breath from distended nostrils.

The youngest rider was seventy-eight, the oldest eighty-four.

'They have a choir of men singers here,' the taxi driver told me on our way home. 'Every man is over a hundred.'

For a fraction of a second I had looked into the darkness beyond my window straight into the wide open eyes of a man not a foot away. He had white eyebrows.

'I wonder have the members of that choir ever walked these roads at night?' I said.

'I doubt it,' said the taxi driver.

NOTE ON WEIGHTS, MEASURES
AND MONEY

THE imperial system of weights and measures used in the
original articles has been retained. Approximate equivalents
are as follows:

Length
1 inch = 25 mm
1 foot = 30 cm
1 yard = 0.9 m
1 mile = 1.6 km

Area
1 acre = 0.4 ha
1 square mile = 2.6 km²

Weight
1 pound = 454 g
1 ton = 1 t

Volume
1 gallon = 4.5 l

Money
There were 12 pennies (d) in 1 shilling, and 20 shillings in 1
pound (£) also called a quid. A guinea was £1. 1s. A shilling
was often called a 'bob', two shillings and sixpence 'half a
crown', a pound a 'sovereign' and five pounds a 'fiver'. The
original 1 pound was a gold coin not a bank note.

When decimal currency was adopted in Australia in 1966,
two dollars were equivalent to one pound.

APPENDIX

Kisses a Quid a Piece *Workers' Voice*, 6 August 1938
Rising Champion *Sun News-Pictorial*, 21 July 1934
The Noble Art *Communist Review*, March 1938
'Six sausages is nothing' *Sun News-Pictorial*, 28 May 1938
The Night We had Visitors *Sun News-Pictorial*, 9 September 1939
'What's the time?' *Sun News-Pictorial*, 20 May 1939
Those who Walk this Street *Angry Penguins* 1945
The Old Woman and the Dogs *Herald*, 6 January 1940
I Look Back *Guardian*, 21 December 1966
Australian Picture-Book I *Left Review*, November 1937
Australian Picture-Book II *Left Review*, December 1937
Rattly Bob *Workers' Voice* November 1937
Tomorrow 'Proletarian Picture Book', *Workers' Voice*, 26 February 1938
'We're beginning to think, now' 'Proletarian Picture Book', *Workers Voice*, 2 July 1938 (pseud. Steve Kennedy)
It won't always be so 'Proletarian Picture Book', *Workers' Voice*, 9 July 1938 (pseud. Steve Kennedy)
Guns for Children 'Proletarian Picture Book' *Workers' Voice*, 29 January 1938
The Dark People *This Land of ours . . . Australia* (ed. George Farwell and Frank H. Johnston), Angus and Robertson, 1949
I wonder what he thinks about *Sun News-Pictorial*, 3 January 1949

Men of the Cattle Country *Walkabout*, 1 November 1951

The Diver *National Times*, 6 January 1979

'There's a dark man in your palm, Lady', *The Territorian*, December 1964

Alan Marshall Discusses His Wooden Friends *Herald*, 9 September 1939

Any Messages for the A.I.F.? *A.B.C. Weekly*, 26 September 1942

The Three Wise Men *Herald*, 24 December 1943

Hallucination before Departure *The Bulletin*, 23 December 1980

Delirium *Angry Penguins*, December 1944

The Little Black Bottle *Sun News-Pictorial*, 23 June 1934

Story-telling. A talk entitled 'Some Aspects of the Writer's Craft' given to the South Australian English Teachers' Association and reprinted in *Opinion* (Journal of South Australian English Teachers' Association), August 1966

A Sense of Wonder, Address at Melbourne University on admission to the honorary degree of Doctor of Laws, 16 December 1972

The Horsemen of Inner Mongolia, *China through Australian Eyes*, New Democratic Publications, 1973

Death Comes to a Mammoth *Age*, 9 January 1965

Horses and Poets of Abkhazia *Age*, 4 December 1964

1